On Capital Punishment

by

William H. Baker

9838

MOODY PRESS
CHICAGO

© 1973, 1985 by
THE MOODY BIBLE INSTITUTE
OF CHICAGO

All Scripture quotations in this book are from the *New American Standard Bible,* except where indicated otherwise.

Library of Congress Cataloging in Publication Data

Baker, William H., 1930-
  On capital punishment.

  Originally published: Worthy of death. c1973.
  Bibliography: p.
  Includes indexes.
  1. Capital punishment—Religious aspects. I. Baker,
William H., 1930-   Worthy of death.   II. Title.
HV8694.B35   1985   261.8′3366   85-4850
ISBN 0-8024-6060-7 (pbk.)

1 2 3 4 5 6 7 Printing/BC/Year 90 89 88 87 86 85

Printed in the United States of America

Contents

TO
my wife,
who first suggested this subject
and provided most of the encouragement
to carry it through

Introduction

On June 29, 1972, the United States Supreme Court ruled that the death penalty, as it had been imposed, was "cruel and unusual" punishment. This decision was hailed by many as a milestone in man's advance toward a more civilized and humane society.

This particular decision involved the case of Furman versus Georgia, so labeled because the lead-off defendant in a group of defendants was named Furman. It was really the climax of efforts by the Legal Defense Fund of the National Association for the Advancement of Colored People, which had gained a moratorium on the death penalty in 1968.

The result of the Furman decision was to set in motion new legislation among many state legislatures that would bring capital punishment statutes into compliance with the Furman decision, for that decision had not suspended the death penalty entirely but merely invalidated current practices.

This process was culminated in 1976 by another landmark decision by the High Court in the case of Gregg versus Georgia. This judgment upheld the death penalty in general as well as certain specific statutes providing for its application.

Other state legislatures now had a model by which they could confidently enact new legislation. What this resulted in, to be specific, were capital punishment statutes that narrowed the kinds of crimes punishable by death and set rigid standards that greatly circumscribed the discretion of judges and juries.

One would think that all problems had been solved, but this is not the case. The trouble is—and it seems to have focused on the Supreme Court—that new issues keep getting raised in individual cases by defense attorneys as to just how the death penalty can be imposed. The result is that very few executions have actually taken place since 1968. Thus *Newsweek* summed it up in its July 18, 1983, issue:

> The Burger court has become America's life-and-death tribunal. No other Supreme Court in history has been as preoccupied with—or bedeviled by—the questions of when life begins and when a state may snuff one out.

Justice William Rehnquist complained: "What troubles me is the Court . . . has made it virtually impossible for states to enforce with reasonable promptness their constitutionally valid capital punishment statutes."[1]

All this points to the fact that the controversy is very much alive and that evangelical Christians should decide on their own position in this vital moral issue so that they can speak, act, and vote in accordance with their biblical perspective.

This book is primarily concerned, therefore, with the biblical teaching on the subject of capital punishment. The answer to the question *Is the death penalty right?*

---

1. *Newsweek* 102 (18 July 1983):56.

must come from the realm of a biblically oriented theology. In his anthology on the subject of capital punishment, Grant McClellan admits:

> The best defense of capital punishment still rests, at the deepest level, on a religious foundation. . . . If man, even collectively as the state, takes another life, questions about the sacredness of life are raised, no matter how heinous a crime the individual may have committed against another individual or society.[2]

Over one hundred years ago, George Cheever said: "Religious and theological considerations enter into its very nature, and none but the most shallow disputants would ever imagine that it could be discussed as it ought to be discussed, on any lower grounds."[3]

Yet today the issue is usually debated on purely humanistic grounds. Such grounds involve the issues of whether the death penalty really deters murder, the fact that there is no possibility of rehabilitating the murderer, the question of society's right to take life, and the belief that capital punishment is inhumane. Although these are important issues, another question is either overlooked or regarded as irrelevant: Is the death penalty *just?*

The question of justice has been set aside simply because such things are looked upon these days as purely relative; that is, society itself determines what is just or unjust, good or bad, right or wrong. Since, then, justice is merely a matter of one's point of view, the issue of capital punishment must be debated on more concrete grounds.

On Capital Punishment is a reminder that justice is, in fact, a matter of divine pronouncement, and that the divine pronouncement is found in the Bible. Such a con-

---

2. Grant S. McClellan, *Capital Punishment* (New York: H. W. Wilson, 1961), p. 3.
3. George B. Cheever, *A Defense of Capital Punishment* (New York: Waley & Putnam, 1846), p. 3.

cept as this is not popular, because it implies a supreme Lawgiver to whom men are accountable.

This book is limited in its scope. It will deal primarily with the principle of capital punishment for malicious and premeditated murder only. The question of degrees of murder and the use of the death penalty for other crimes such as kidnapping are beyond its scope.

Capital punishment may be defined as "the execution of a criminal under death sentence imposed by competent public authority."[4] The term *capital punishment* is taken from the Latin *caput,* a word used by the Romans variously to mean the head, the life, or the civil rights of an individual. Basically, then, *capital* carries the idea of "chief," "principal," or "extreme" penalty.

Those who oppose the death penalty have been far more active and militant in their efforts than those who support it. This is easy to understand, since it is difficult, except out of a desire for revenge, to champion a cause that leads to peoples' deaths. Thus the opponents to capital punishment come off looking like humane, courageous advocates of life. But their arguments often smack of sentimentalism, not clear logic.

Defending the idea of capital punishment must be low-keyed and unemotional. Nevertheless, if polls mean anything, the majority of Americans favor the death penalty. This arises out of the public's perception that murder is on the increase and that relatively few executions are directly to blame.

Many sincere Christians oppose capital punishment on what they believe are biblical grounds. *On Capital Punishment* is concerned mainly with this form of opposition, and its appeal to biblical material is an attempt to provide Christians with more data by which they can take a position on a very relevant and serious moral issue.

---

4. *New Catholic Encyclopedia,* s.v. "Capital Punishment."

Part 1
Historical Survey
of Capital Punishment

1
Earliest Times

If one assumes that the book of Genesis was written by
Moses, it constitutes the earliest record of the institution of capital punishment. Genesis 9:6 says, "Whoever
sheds man's blood, By man his blood shall be shed."
Later we will deal with the question of the relation of
Genesis 9:6 to organized government, which actually
came later, but clearly the earliest practice of this mandate was in the custom of the "avenger of blood," which
continued until Mosaic times and required the nearest
relative to execute vengeance upon the murderer of his
kin (Num. 35:12).

Despite the purpose of Genesis 9:6, the execution of
justice was not the sole motive in the minds of those who
sought to avenge their brethren in early times, nor were
they always careful to ascertain the guilt or innocence of
their victims. Often, revenge was strictly a matter of self-
defense, a reflex action. It sought to destroy what constituted a menace, but it contained a rough idea of justice—
that no one can intrude upon the rights of another without suffering the consequences.

Prehistoric Times

In prehistoric society, vengeance often rested among families and tribes. Among the Bantu tribes, for instance, a murderer proved guilty was given over to the relatives of his victim to deal with him as they saw fit. Sometimes a whole clan or tribe would put to death or banish a man who made himself a nuisance to everyone. Occasionally an entire Eskimo village would rise against and slay an atrocious murderer.

As a rule, capital punishment was meted out in primitive society for such crimes as sorcery, murder, incest, treason, sacrilege, adultery, and theft. In some tribes a person was put to death only for sorcery, murder, and adultery. However, some despotic kingdoms in Africa punished even small offenses by death, at the capricious will of the chief.

Murder was almost universally believed to be a horrible crime, and in some tribes it was extremely rare. But generally this view was restricted to the tribe or clan, and murder was regarded as harmless or praiseworthy outside those limits.

Thus, the original divine requirement to punish the murderer with death became corrupted by the descendants of Noah to mean only an act of defense against a source of danger to the group. The murderer was regarded as being infected with the uncleanness of death or surrounded by evil spirits and especially the spirit of his victim, who would afflict him and others as well if he went unpunished.

Did capital punishment occur before Noah? There seems to be no historical record of such a thing, especially if a date of 5000 B.C. can be assigned to him. Some see in the words of Lamech (Gen. 4:24), "If Cain is avenged sevenfold, Then Lamech seventy-sevenfold," an indication that death was regarded as the fitting punishment for murder, but this is by no means an example of capital punishment.

EARLY CIVILIZATIONS

The earliest records of the death sentence are those of the Bible, the Code of Hammurabi, and the Babylonian codes of laws (in fragments only). During Assyrio-Babylonian times, the death penalty was exacted for false accusation of killing. The ancient Hittites reserved death mainly for crimes committed by slaves or crimes against the king. The death penalty was usually not inflicted for theft unless it involved the stripping of deities and temples. One strange code indicates that the death penalty was inflicted on a man who sold or bought property without proper witnesses or contracts, perhaps the reflection of false pretenses in receiving it, but at any rate a reflection of the high value placed upon property by the Assyrians and Babylonians. Other crimes entailing the death penalty were failure to make restitution after theft, kidnapping a freeborn child, negligence that proved fatal, infidelity, and incest. There is a record of a "wine woman" in a public house being required to assist in apprehending a criminal or suffering the death penalty.

One historian claims that the earliest (about 1500 B.C.) recorded death sentence of any of the early civilizations has been found in Egypt. In this case a criminal was found guilty of "magic" but was left to inflict the punishment upon himself as his own executioner![1]

In the Far East, the Chinese put to death those guilty of murder, piracy, highway robbery, rebellion, counterfeiting, forgery, arson, rape of girls under twelve, fraud at public examination, and smuggling salt.

In Japan, very little can be learned, because of the mixture of myth, legend, and chronicle that took the place of history in that land for hundreds of years, except that there seems to have been a staff of executioners who administered capital punishment by decapitation.

---

1 John Laurence, *A History of Capital Punishment* (New York: Citadel, 1960), p. 2.

During Homeric times, the Greeks believed in the power of the spirit of the murdered man to exact vengeance. Outside of this, however, the murderer was under no disability, so long as he kept outside the range of the clan among which the murder was committed. If he should venture within their reach, though, his life was forfeit to the kinsmen of the murdered man, who were bound to exact the blood penalty, especially if they themselves wished to avoid the wrath of the dead man's ghost.

In Athenian times, punishment no longer depended on the individual avenger but on the state. The penalty of death followed conviction along with the confiscation of goods. However, killing a noncitizen was punishable by banishment. Trials were held in the open air and at a temple, the usual places of asylum. The accused could withdraw himself from the trial not later than the conclusion of his opening speech, and, so long as he remained abroad, his life was protected; but, if he returned to Athens, he could be put to death with impunity.

In Sparta, capital offenses that had been acquitted could be tried again. In Athens, murder, defacing coins, certain cases of theft, kidnapping, and pickpocketing were capital crimes.

Among Jews, despite the provisions of Mosaic law, the Talmudic authorities seem to have been convinced that it was not within the province of human beings to punish other human beings by taking life; only God had that right. However, they could not override the biblical command or set it aside completely by another kind of punishment. Instead they interpreted the biblical law by making legal restrictions so numerous that it became virtually impossible to impose a death sentence.[2] Jews were torn between their respect for biblical authority, which commanded the death penalty, and their own con-

---

2. Hyman E. Goldin, *Hebrew Criminal Law and Procedure* (New York: Twayne, 1952), p. 24.

viction that they were not qualified to pass such judgment. This tension gave rise to many conflicting statements in the Talmud regarding capital punishment. Eventually, of course, the Jewish courts lost to the Roman government the right of deciding capital cases, though historians are not agreed as to when this actually took place.

Every precaution was taken by the Jews to safeguard the rights of the convicted man and avoid a possible mistake. For example, the rabbis kept the interval between sentence and execution to a minimum, and as the condemned man was led to the place of execution, a herald would precede the procession to proclaim the criminal's name and offense and request that anyone having information bearing upon the case step forward and present it. Should this information be forthcoming, the criminal would then be returned to court, which remained in session throughout the execution, and the evidence would be considered.

THE ROMAN ERA

During the republican era in Rome, capital punishment was rare and was imposed mainly for crimes among the military. The *lex talionis,* the law of retaliation, was embraced by the Law of the Twelve Tables (450 B.C.). Under the empire, both the number of crimes as well as the cases of capital punishment gradually increased. The Romans considered capital punishment to be a deterrent, thus victims were usually punished publicly by crucifixion, burning, and decapitation. Under Nero, victims were impaled and often suffered death in the arena. Polybius refers to the Roman practice of exile in place of death, a choice given to those found guilty.[3]

There was an ancient debate between Caesar and Cato,

---

3. Polybius *The Histories* 6.14.

recorded by Sallust, in which some of the arguments against capital punishment sound strangely contemporary. They were: (1) innocent men are sometimes punished; (2) if the extreme penalty is required, why not add torture? (3) does not severe punishment win sympathy for the criminal? (4) is death, in fact, a punishment? and (5) is the death penalty necessary to protect society from criminals?[4] Many modern advocates of the abolition of capital punishment who consider their crusade innovative should take notice that their ideas are centuries old.

Outside the Roman empire, among the Teutonic and Slavic peoples, the penalty of death was usually decreed by the public assembly, though banishment was often substituted, according to Tacitus. There is some debate as to whether or not capital punishment among the Germanic tribes may have served the function of appeasing the wrath of the gods.[5]

Among the Celts, when human sacrifices were made, criminals were sacrificed before the innocent victims, a practice reflecting, perhaps, the feeling that certain forms of behavior were considered to be displeasing to the gods. In Irish law a few circumstances called for the death penalty as such. Welsh law has a few allusions to the penalty of hanging for theft.

---

4 Sallust *Conspiracy of Catiline* 51.22.40.
5 See Folke Strom, *On the Origin of the German Death Penalties* (Stockholm: Wahtstrom & Widstrand, 1942), pp. 1-330.

2
The Christian Era

The biblical writers will not be considered as such at this point, since this book will seek during the second part to build its arguments on what I consider a biblically oriented theology. At this point, we shall consider how the writers of the New Testament were interpreted by the early church Fathers, who lived very close to the same situation but can provide a historical basis for the biblical discussion later.

THE EARLY CHURCH PERIOD

The church Fathers who lived during the first four centuries were not always clear in their teaching about capital punishment. Tertullian is considered by one authority to have been unequivocal in his opposition to taking of life without exception,[1] but the following passage could leave some doubt, since it quotes Romans 13:4 and implies the right of the state to take life:

1 *New Catholic Encyclopedia*, s.v. "Capital Punishment."

No doubt the apostle admonishes the Romans to be subject to all power, because there is no power but of God, and because (the ruler) does not carry the Sword without reason, and is the servant of God, nay also, says he, a revenger to execute wrath upon him that doeth evil. . . . Thus he bids you be subject to the powers, not on an opportunity occurring for avoiding martyrdom, but when he is making an appeal in behalf of a good life, under the view also of their being as it were handmaids of the divine court of justice, even here pronounces sentence beforehand upon the guilty.[2]

Lactantius is much more clear in his feelings:

For when God forbids us to kill, He not only prohibits us from open violence, which is not even allowed by the public laws, but He warns us against the commission of those things which are esteemed lawful among men. . . . It makes no difference whether you put a man to death by word, or rather by the sword, since it is the act of putting to death itself which is prohibited. Therefore, with regard to the precept of God, there ought to be no exception at all; but that it is always unlawful to put to death a man, whom God willed to be a sacred animal.[3]

Augustine, who set the pattern for many things which followed in the Middle Ages, defended capital punishment for the sake of social order, but praised the Christian instinct to temper such juridical sternness. Commenting on Romans 13:4 he says: " 'For he beareth not the sword in vain,' saith the apostle. Draw not the sword wherewith thou dost strike Christ. . . . The authority is

2. Tertullian, "Scorpiace," in *The Ante-Nicene Fathers*, ed. A. Roberts and J. Donaldson, trans. S. Thelwall (New York: Scribner, 1899), 3:647.
3. Lactantius, "The Divine Institutes," in *The Ante-Nicene Fathers*, ed. A. Roberts and J. Donaldson, trans. William Fletcher (New York: Scribner, 1913), 7:187.

hated because it is legitimate; he acts in a hated manner who acts according to the law."[4]

In his greatest work, *The City of God*, Augustine refers to the right of the state:

> There are some exceptions made by the divine authority to its own law, that men may not be put to death. These exceptions are of two kinds, being justified either by a general law, or by a special commission granted for a time to some individual. And in this latter case, he to whom the authority is delegated, and who is but the sword in the hand of him who uses it, is not himself responsible for the death he deals.[5]

THE MIDDLE AGES

During the Middle Ages, the number of capital crimes increased, and the mode of inflicting the penalty became increasingly more cruel. From the time of the death of William the Conqueror, the number of executions increased in England, and the value of human life seems to have decreased considerably. Sometimes the church offered sanctuary to the criminal. Some representatives, like the Abbot of Battle Abbey, had the right to spare the life of any condemned, a right granted by William. Late during this period in England, a statute was enacted that virtually granted immunity to the clergy. Anyone could claim benefit of clergy and was examined as to his "scholarship." This consisted of his reading a passage, usually Psalm 51, which became known as the "neck verse." Abuse of this became so widespread that after 1487 the privilege of clergy was allowed only after a first

4. Augustine *On the Gospel of John* (*Nicene and Post-Nicene Fathers,* 1st ser., ed. Philip Schaff, trans. John Gibb and James Innes [New York: Scribner, 1900], 3:35), tractate 5.12.
5. Augustine *The City of God* (*Basic Writings of Saint Augustine,* ed. Whitney J. Oates [New York: Random, 1948], 2:28) 1.21.

conviction This privilege, of course, did not extend to heretics, who were burned alive.

Among the churchmen, those who spoke against the church's becoming involved in capital punishment were Pope Leo I in the fifth century and Nicholas I in the ninth. Councils such as Toledo (675) and the Fourth Lateran (1215) forbade clerics to take any part in a juridical process or sentence on a capital charge.

The leading Catholic theologian, Thomas Aquinas, spoke in the following manner regarding capital punishment:

> Therefore if a man be dangerous and infectious to the community, on account of some sin, it is praiseworthy and advantageous that he be killed in order to safeguard the common good, since *a little leaven corrupteth the whole lump* (I Cor. v. 6). . . . It is lawful to kill an evildoer in so far as it is directed to the welfare of the whole community so that it belongs to him alone who has charge of the community's welfare. . . . Now the care of the common good is entrusted to persons of rank having public authority: wherefore they alone, and not private individuals, can lawfully put evildoers to death.[6]

THE REFORMATION PERIOD

The attitude toward capital punishment changed little during Reformation times. In fact, Henry VIII created a record for execution and legalized death by boiling in 1531. The burning of witches, which had started in the fifteenth century in England, continued into the eighteenth century.

6. St. Thomas Aquinas *Summa Theologica* (trans. Fathers of the English Dominican Province [New York: Benziger Brothers, 1947], 2:1467) 64:2.

Martin Luther had this advice to give to a ruler during a revolt of peasants:

> I will not oppose a ruler who, even though he does not tolerate the Gospel, will smite and punish these peasants without offering to submit the case to judgment. For he is within his rights, since the peasants are not contending any longer for the Gospel. . . . whom even heathen rulers have the right and power to punish; nay, it is their duty to punish them, for it is just for this purpose that they bear the sword, and are "the ministers of God upon him that doeth evil."[7]

John Calvin took a firm stand for capital punishment. In answer to the question How can magistrates be pious men and shedders of blood at the same time? he said:

> Yet if we understand that the magistrate in administering punishments does nothing by himself, but carries out the very judgments of God, we shall not be hampered by this scruple. The law of the Lord forbids killing; but, that murderers may not go unpunished, the Lawgiver himself puts into the hand of his ministers a sword to be drawn against all murderers. It is not for the pious to afflict and hurt; yet to avenge, at the Lord's command, the afflictions of the pious is not to hurt or to afflict.[8]

In his commentary on Romans 13:4, Calvin had this to say:

> This is a noteworthy passage for proving the right of the sword. If by arming the magistrate the Lord has also com-

---

7. Martin Luther, "Against the Robbing and Murdering Peasants," in *The Works of Martin Luther* (Philadelphia: Muhlenberg, 1931), 4:251.
8. John Calvin, *Institutes of the Christian Religion,* ed. John T. McNeill, trans. Ford L. Battles (Philadelphia: Westminster, 1965), 2:1497.

mitted to him the use of the sword, then whenever he
punishes the guilty by death, he is obeying God's commands by exercising His vengeance. Those, therefore,
who consider that it is wrong to shed the blood of the
guilty are contending against God.[9]

Though the voices of Luther and Calvin can be considered predominant during the time of the Reformation,
there were other voices even at this time calling for the
abolition of capital punishment on alleged Christian
bases. Even though the Anabaptists, for example, were
somewhat divided on the issue, it appears that the pre-
vailing conviction among them was that magistrates
should abandon the use of the sword in the punishment
not only of religious dissenters, but also of common
criminals.[10] The founding leader of the Mennonites,
Menno Simons, had this to say of worldly rulers' practice:

> There are some sins, as for instance murder, witchcraft,
> incendiarism, theft, and other like criminal deeds, which
> eventually require and imply punishment at the hands of
> the magistracy. . . . Therefore act with discretion, and do
> not judge such matters involving capital punishment, es-
> pecially if they are public, as you would other works of the
> flesh which do not constitute an offence and cause for
> reproach in the eyes of the world.[11]

However, in relation to the Christian ruler, he considered
it wrong to "shed blood" in hope that the criminal might
repent and accept Christ and "in the light of the compas-

9. John Calvin, "The Epistles of Paul the Apostle to the Romans and
   to the Thessalonians," in *Calvin's Commentaries,* trans. Ross Mac-
   kenzie (Grand Rapids: Eerdmans, 1960), p. 283.
10. Robert Kreider, "Anabaptists and the State," in *The Recovery of the
    Anabaptist Vision,* ed. G. F. Hershberger (Scottdale, Pa.: Herald,
    1957), p. 192.
11. Menno Simons, "Instruction on Discipline of the Church at Fran-
    eker (1555)," in *The Complete Writings of Menno Simons,* ed. J. C.
    Wenger, trans. Verduin (Scottdale, Pa.: Herald, 1956), p. 1043.

sionate, merciful kind nature . . . and example of Christ . . . which example he has commanded all His chosen children to follow."[12]

12. Menno Simons, "Reply to Martin Micron," in *The Complete Writings of Menno Simons,* pp. 920-22.

3
The Modern Era

The modern era, beginning roughly in the seventeenth century with the rise of science and humanism, is largely an era in which movements for abolition of the death penalty have made their impact upon penal thinking. In England executions became more and more brutal, and this added fuel to the fires of abolition. There, for example, the practice of hanging, drawing, and quartering became common during the reign of Elizabeth, and Lord Coke found justification for great brutality in a collection of Bible texts—a practice that came to be known as "godly butchery." In England and the Irish Free State, there was no distinction between minors and adults, and many children were executed for relatively minor crimes. However, as the result of efforts for reform, England finally eliminated over one hundred ninety capital offenses in 1860.

Cesare Beccaria is directly responsible for influencing the modern reform movement in penology. In 1764 he wrote an essay entitled "On Crime and Punishment," which was based on his theory of society. His challenge probably led to the abolition of capital punishment in Tuscany (1786) and in Austria (1787). He also directly influenced Samuel Romilly and others to reform the English penal code and reduce the number of capital offenses. Beccaria cited only one justifiable reason, in his opinion, for capital punishment: when a person threatens the existence of the state.[1] Historian William Lecky has this to say of Beccaria's influence:

> The reform of the law in England, as over the rest of Europe, may ultimately be traced to that Voltarian school of which Baccaria was the chief representative, for the impulse created by his treatise "On Crime and Punishment" was universal, and it was the first great effort to infuse a spirit of philanthropy into the penal code, making it a main object of legislation to inflict the smallest amount of suffering.[2]

Along with Beccaria in Italy, others like Voltaire and Rousseau in France; Savigny, Marx, and Kelsen in Germany; Hume and Bentham in England; and Franklin and Paine in America made a concerted attack upon the Christian philosophy that undergirded Western civilization. This included the Western concept of justice and morality in the punishment of crime. Biblical justice was cast aside as medieval and barbaric.

The efforts for abolition were not exerted among skeptics and infidels alone. George Fox, founder of Quakerism, while in prison at Derby in 1650-51, saw the inequity of the criminal law that put men to death for petty theft, and he began his crusade to reform English penal

---

1. Cesare Beccaria, "On Crime and Punishment," in *An Essay on Crimes and Punishments,* trans. E. D. Ingraham (Stanford: Academic Reprints, 1952), p. 98.
2. William Lecky, *The Rise and Influence of Rationalism in Europe* (London: Longmans, Green, 1910), 2:349.

law and abolish capital punishment. Another Quaker, John Bellers, wrote an essay in 1714 entitled "Some Reasons Against Putting of Felons to Death," in an effort to reform criminal law in England. Later, Elizabeth Fry, also a Quaker, wrote:

> But is it for man to take the prerogative of the Almighty into his own hands? Is it not his place rather to endeavor to reform such or to restrain them from the commission of further evil? At least to afford poor erring fellow-mortals, whatever may be their offenses, an opportunity of proving their repentance by amendment of life.[3]

Finally, just before the days of reform, Quakers William Allen and Peter Bedford worked for more humane criminal procedure and the abolition of capital punishment in England.

In 1840 the first attempt was made in Parliament to abolish capital punishment, but it failed. However, great reforms did take place in the prisons a few years later.

During this period on the Continent, before the influence of the abolitionists took hold, capital punishment became more inhumane and degrading. In Germany some victims in the army were hunted and speared to death. In Russia, running the gauntlet and flogging to death were common. And in France capital sentences were accompanied by prolonged torture. In Sweden in 1734, capital punishment was inflicted for sixty-eight crimes. Beginning in 1870 when Holland abolished capital punishment, many other countries began to do so also, so that today the majority of them no longer use the death penalty, except, in some cases, for treason or crimes against the state.

3. Leonard S. Kenworthy, ed., *Quaker Leaders Speak* (Philadephia: Friends Book Store, 1952), p. 54. On p. 49, editor Kenworthy says: "The modern movement for the humane treatment of prisoners is due in large part to the efforts of Elizabeth Fry, a sensitive, imaginative, and courageous English Quaker."

DEVELOPMENTS OF THE TWENTIETH CENTURY

It is not within the scope of this book to go into the details of more recent developments in England and America. However, the following summary will be appropriate.

At the turn of the century three countercurrents favored retention and reinstitution of capital punishment, which temporarily turned the tide of abolition. The first might be called a "conservative" movement. This was the result of an increase of crime in England and the Continent during the closing years of the nineteenth century, which aroused public opinion in favor of capital punishment. The second was more scientific and was the result of the publishing of two works, *Criminal Man* by Lombroso and *Criminology* by Garofalo. The former book suggested the idea of a man biologically and psychologically destined to commit crime, whereas the latter introduced the concept of social dangerousness. These works led to the feeling that the humanitarianism and sentimentalism of judges and juries must be opposed. The third development was totalitarianism, or authoritarianism, which arose in Europe in the form of German national socialism and Italian fascism, as extreme examples. This was the idea that authoritarian regimes, produced by revolution, should be defended by all available means.

Following World War II, the abolitionist movement received new life by a reaction to totalitarianism and by such things as the Universal Declaration of Human Rights (1948). Italy, for example, returned to the Beccarian tradition, and Germany excluded capital punishment by constitutional provision. In England, a considerable amount of literature, two abolitionist victories in the House of Commons, and the effects of the work of the Royal Commission resulted in the compromise Homicide Act of 1957, which reduced capital crimes, distinguished between capital and noncapital murder, and introduced the concept of limited responsibility.

In 1968 in the United States a moratorium was declared on capital punishment, and in 1972 the Supreme Court (Furman vs. Georgia) struck down the states' existing death penalty statutes and sent the legislatures back to a re-formulation of their laws. Clarification came in 1976 (Gregg vs. Georgia), and further revision had to be made by many states. The appeals process has made it difficult to execute anyone, and as of October 1983, 1,230 convicts were still on death row.

But a Supreme Court decision of July 6, 1983, could speed up the appeals process by employing a new procedure used by the federal appeals court in New Orleans. This may make the convicts on death row closer to execution.

As of July 1983, thirty-eight states had capital punishment statutes, New Jersey being the latest addition. The trend seems to be toward the addition of states, for in 1982 thirty-five states had the death penalty.[4]

Since 1977 when the Supreme Court (Everheart vs. Georgia) ruled that rape and kidnapping do not warrant death, only murder and treason have been grounds for taking life.

POSITIONS OF THE RELIGIOUS BODIES

To close this chapter, a few comments are in order as to the position of various religious bodies on capital punishment, since this book will deal with the theological issues.

JUDAISM

The Jewish view of capital punishment is a combination of the Old Testament, the Mishnah, and the Gemara,

4. *U.S. News and World Report,* vol. 95, no. 21 (18 July 1983).

plus the development of many centuries. Since biblical law was considered to be divinely revealed, it could not be completely abrogated. In order to surmount this obstacle, the rabbis had to resort to legal technicalities that had the effect of making the biblical law unenforceable. Jewish sentiment against capital punishment may still be expressed as it was by the Mishnah: a court that executes one man in seven years is a "destructive" one; or, perhaps, as R. Eleazar ben Azariah put it more strongly, one execution in seventy years is too much.[5]

ROMAN CATHOLICS

Relatively few Roman Catholics in the United States or elsewhere have been active in debates over capital punishment. When Catholic theologians have dealt with the topic, they have tended to repeat affirmations of the state's right to inflict the death penalty, especially for the reasons of social defense and deterrence. However, Pius XII, in his extensive statements on crime and punishment, never explicitly defended or denied the state's right to impose the death sentence, though he defended its right to have retributive intentions in its penal administration. John XXIII's ideas on the inalienable rights of the human person set forth in his *Pacem in Terris* may very likely set the tone for current Catholic pronouncements.

In 1983, Pope John Paul II called for "clemency and mercy for those condemned to death, especially those who have been condemned for political motives,"[6] which seems to reflect a growing Catholic attitude, even

5. Cited by Israel J. Kazis, "Judaism and the Death Penalty," in *The Death Penalty in America*, ed. Hugo Adam Bedau (Chicago: Aldine, 1964), p. 171.
6. Quoted by William F. Buckley in "War Against Capital Punishment," *National Review* 35, no. 207 (18 February 1983).

among conservatives like John Paul II. In 1980 the Catholic bishops officially opposed capital punishment.

PROTESTANTS

Among Protestants there is considerable disagreement on the topic of capital punishment, as might be expected. Liberal churchmen are fairly well unified, however, in their opposition to the death penalty, and they probably constitute the majority. Among evangelicals there is a cleavage on the issue, but it can be said that among the stricter fundamentalists where a greater stress is placed on the literal or normal interpretation of Scripture, there is general unanimity in favor of the retention of the death penalty.

Both liberal and evangelical churchmen who oppose capital punishment do so along these lines: (1) punishment should be to protect society by deterring crime and rehabilitating the criminal—the death penalty does neither; (2) the death penalty discriminates against the poor, the uneducated, and the black; (3) the fear of executing an innocent man stalks the conscience of many a legal official; (4) the delay that comes as a result of appeals and deliberation nullifies its effect as a deterrent to crime; and (5) capital punishment cannot be reconciled with the love of God, thus society must seek redemption of evildoers. As to this last argument, evangelicals usually feel obliged to prove that the clear teaching for capital punishment in the Old Testament has been superseded in the New Testament by the teachings of Jesus and the principle of grace.

In a more practical manner, Senator Mark Hatfield of Oregon, an evangelical Christian, has been quoted as being opposed to the death penalty because it cannot be administered justly under the present jury system.[7]

7 "After Capital Punishment, What?" *United Evangelical Action* 24 (May 1965): 17.

Charles Colson, a "born-again" Christian of Watergate fame, objects on the grounds that Numbers 35:29-30 requires two "eyewitnesses" for *any* conviction, and Deuteronomy 17:7 requires that these witnesses be participants in the execution, neither of which is observed in today's legal processes.[8]

The liberal voice of Protestantism, *Christian Century,* has engaged in a crusade to abolish capital punishment for more than three decades. One contributor, Dane R. Gordon, is typical:

> On the one hand, it is felt that punishment should be equal to the offense, that as the most serious wrongdoing, murder, should bring the most severe penalty—death. On the other hand, there is the strong belief that life is unique, sacred, that . . . society accepts a terrible responsibility when it deprives any person of his life—even when he has taken the life of another. . . . It can be argued that an injury done to one member of the human family is felt, directly or indirectly, by all members of the family. They all are responsible for the process not only of punishing but of healing and reconstructing. The person who committed the crime is also a member of the human family. To put him to death is to absolve him forever from responsibility to repair the damage he has done. He is "let off" not when his life is spared, but when he is put to death—and the responsibility which should have been his falls on those who remain. Thus society is injured twice—first by the crime, again when relieving the guilty one of responsibility.[9]

As a result of such campaigns to abolish capital punishment, the following Protestant religious bodies have taken a public stand against the death penalty: American Unitarian Association (1956), Church of the Brethren

---

8. Cited by Marshall Shelley in "The Death Penalty: Two Sides of a Growing Issue," *Christianity Today* 28 (2 March 1984): 14-17.
9. Dane R. Gordon, "Justice and the Death Penalty," *Christian Century* 80, no. 27 (3 July 1963): 955.

(1957), Christian Church (Disciples—1957, 1962, 1973), Universalist Church of America (1957), Anglican Church of Canada's Executive Council (1958), Protestant Episcopal Church in the U.S. (1958), United Presbyterian Church in the U.S. (1959, 1977), American Baptist Churches (1960, 1977), American Ethical Union (1960), United Methodist Church (1960, 1976), United Church of Canada (1960), National Council of Churches (1968, 1976), United Church of Christ (1969, 1977), American Lutheran Church (1972), American Friends Service Committee (1976), and Friends Committee on National Legislation (1977).

Conclusion

This historical survey has traced the practice of capital punishment from its institution in Genesis 9:6 to the present day. It is clear that the divisions of opinion that have existed have not been between religious people and nonreligious people, for both classes alike have opposed and approved the death penalty for various reasons. Individual Christians have made their appeals from the Bible for both abolition and retention. An individual's position on this issue may or may not be derived from Scripture, as history has demonstrated. A determination of just what the Scriptures actually teach will be one of the endeavors of this book.

The Great Mandate
for Capital Punishment

4
The Mandate in Genesis 9:6

The growing abhorrence toward the death penalty that has occurred over the last few centuries has often been the result of purely emotional experiences and a growing humanistic tendency. However, one of the earliest attempts to establish an objective basis for abolishing capital punishment was a question raised in the area of the right of government to take life.

ALTERNATIVE EXPLANATIONS

One frequently leveled charge is that capital punishment is no more than legalized murder. In 1764 Cesare Beccaria, who had such a great impact on penal reform, wrote, "Is it not absurd, that the laws, which detest and punish homicide, should, in order to prevent murder, publicly commit murder themselves?"[1] Usually, of course, this charge takes the form in which a distinction

1. Cesare Beccaria, "On Crime and Punishment," in *An Essay on Crimes and Punishments,* trans. E. D. Ingraham (Stanford: Academic Reprints, 1952), 104-5.

between murder with malice and the act of the executioner is recognized. In this case, society itself becomes the "murderer," and no particular grievance is aimed at the executioner himself or to the judge and jury who pronounced the death sentence.

To justify further the charge of legalized murder, some psychologists go so far as to suggest that even in the due process of law there are the elements of vengeance and the desire to give vent to "hostility feelings." It is true that such feelings are expressed by some members of society. They are directed at criminal scapegoats who offer the least threat to their security and standing as good citizens. Capital punishment is placed into this process as "an intense expression of deflected hostility."[2] Those who make this claim fail to recognize the need for capital punishment as a due process of law in order to control popular passions, which exist in every society. Neither do they say much about the inherent sense of justice that inspires people to take the law into their own hands when they fear the possible failure of constituted authority to administer justice. Are these feelings to be discredited entirely, or is there a legitimate basis for them?

Finally, some allege that the state's assumption of the right to take life is an assumption of the prerogative of God. This often involves the idea of human fallibility and the consequent possibility of a miscarriage of justice by putting to death an innocent victim, which will be dealt with later. It is characteristic of those who argue thus to make the death penalty sound like the final judgment itself, and the consigning of men to death as the ultimate sentence of eternal perdition, but this is purely emotional nonsense. There is most assuredly a final tribunal for which even condemned murderers can prepare them-

---

2. B. E. Eshelman, "Vengeance and the Law," *Social Action* 22 (April 1961): 26.

selves if they are so inclined. To imply that society, through the courts, condemns a man in such a manner stated above is silly. Capital punishment does not make the nation the final arbiter of a man's destiny. Are those of the Old Testament guilty of violation of the prerogatives of God when they kept the law of capital punishment as stated, for example, in Exodus 21?

There has been, much to the embarrassment of abolitionists, a remarkable amount of assumption among nations throughout history that the state has the right to pass the death penalty, and that this right was absolutely essential to their existence. Those who have made this assumption among nations have always clearly seen the basic difference between the illegality and immorality of private action in taking life and the perfect reasonableness of society to step in with its duly authorized officials to execute those who took private action.

Polybius, the Roman historian (born c. 210 B.C.), may have been unaware of the philosophical or theological reasons for it, but he recognized this right when he wrote:

> For it is the people which alone has the right to confer honours and inflict punishment, the only bonds by which kingdoms and states and in a word human society in general are held together. . . . It is by the people, then, in many cases that offenses punishable by a fine are tried when the accused have held the highest office; and they are the only court which may try on capital charges.[3]

It is the purpose of this chapter to inquire into the origin of this mandate from Scripture and to demonstrate from Scripture that it has continued to be in effect and today remains as the rightful, delegated prerogative of human government. Such an argument, admittedly, will

---

3 Polybius, *The Histories,* 6.14.3.301.

carry weight only for those who accept the authority of the Bible.

Genesis 9:6 is the simplest statement of the mandate for man to punish his fellow man for the crime of murder. "Whoever sheds man's blood, By man his blood shall be shed, For in the image of God He made man." Its very simplicity and lack of development here has been the occasion for opponents of capital punishment to question its extent and relevance to the issue. There is no specific reference to civil government, exceptions, or due process of law. All that is said is that God would require the punishment of the murderer at the hands of another man. Just how far can this simple mandate be carried? Martin Luther is careful to note that basically it is a sharing of authority with man:

> In this passage . . . the Lord establishes a new law and wants murderers to be ruled by men. This was something that had not been customary in the world until now, for God had reserved all judgment for Himself. It was for this reason that He Himself finally exacted punishment from the wicked world by means of the Flood when He saw that the world was daily becoming more and more corrupt. Here, however, God shares His power with man and grants him power over life and death among men, provided that the person is guilty of shedding blood.[4]

The mandate might be regarded as unenforceable, since no clear distinction between willful murder and excusable homicide is made. But this would ignore the fact that the mandate was given to a reasonable man endowed with a conscience, who would be certain to

4. Martin Luther, "Lectures on Genesis," in *The Works of Martin Luther* (Philadelphia: Muhlenberg, 1931), 2:140-41.

recognize such implications and limitations purely from a natural sense of justice. Later on, cities of refuge did not establish for the first time a recognition of accidental or justified homicide but rather were established for the purpose of designating in a growing nation those with whom the responsibility would lie for proper litigation and where the asylum would be.

THE ENDURING NATURE OF THE MANDATE

Genesis 9 marks a distinct turning point in the Mosaic narrative. Noah and his family had been preserved through the cataclysm of the Flood, along with such forms of life as God had directed to be preserved for the new earth. What transpires following this flood as recorded in Genesis 9:1-7 was the establishment of a covenant. Several features of great significance were initiated: the estrangement of animal life from man, permission to eat meat (except for the blood), and the delegation of the death penalty for murder into the hands of man.

Noah stood at the head of a new order of mankind. Though his story is preserved in the Hebrew Scriptures, he was not a Hebrew himself. In fact, he is the direct progenitor of all the human races and nations. What involves him, therefore, involves mankind in general, certainly not Israel alone.

The nature of Genesis 9 is often overlooked by those who feel obliged to minimize its importance and relevance to the subject of capital punishment. Frequently, what was said to Noah is confused with what was given to the nation of Israel, and the impression is conveyed that capital punishment originated with the law of Moses. The Old Testament was given to Israel and was written by Israelites, but the divine history that it represents is not limited to Israel. Granted, the greater part of the historical narrative deals with Israel, and other events are recorded as they relate to and converge upon Israel. But in the attempt to relegate Genesis 9 to a place of relative insignificance, the abolitionist violates good principles of hermeneutics, one of which is a gross indifference to the historical context.

For example, there is the claim that if Genesis 9:6 has any lasting effect, so do all the other practices among the patriarchs, such as taking a slain brother's wife and fathering children of her in her deceased husband's name, a practice which much later became a part of Mosaic law (Deut. 25:5-6).[5] Such a claim ignores the historical context and fails to take into consideration to whom a promise or command was given.

Several factors in the context make clear that the Noahic covenant and the mandate for capital punishment contained in it are enduring: (1) seasons were instituted which continue as a part of the natural order (Gen. 8:22); (2) the dread of man by animals continues as a basic relationship between man and the animal kingdom (Gen. 9:2); (3) the eating of meat is still permitted (Gen. 9:3); (4) no flood has again destroyed the earth (Gen. 9:11), of which the rainbow serves as a continuing pledge (Gen. 9:16-17); and (5) the violation of the image of God continues to be a reason for exacting the extreme penalty (Gen. 9:6). These are factors that man takes for granted but which Scripture clearly identifies as provisions of the Noahic covenant. They are obviously universal in scope, and no subsequent legislation by God or man would have affected them. Later, we will observe that this is indeed the case.

The mandate of Genesis 9:6 is not only an integral part of the order of things instituted in the context, but it is unhindered in continuation. C. F. Keil perceives this when he says:

5. John MacMaster, *The Divine Purpose of Capital Punishment* (London: Kegan Paul, Trench, Trubner, 1892), p. 14.

This command then laid the foundation for all civil government, and formed a necessary complement to that unalterable continuance of the order of nature which had been promised to the human race for its further development. If God on account of the innate sinfulness of man would no more bring an exterminating judgment upon the earthly creation, it was necessary that by commands and authorities He should erect a barrier against the supremacy of evil, and thus lay the foundation for a well-ordered civil development of humanity, in accordance with the words of the blessing, which are repeated in ver. 7, as showing the intention and goal of the new historical beginning.[6]

It would be logical to say that had God begun at some later point to deal with the murderer directly in the form of immediate divine punishment, then man could assume that his responsibility in the matter had ceased. That such is not the case is tacit evidence of the enduring nature of the mandate of Genesis 9:6.

THE BASIS OF HUMAN GOVERNMENT?

There are those who question the validity of assuming that Genesis 9:5-6, with its demand for retributive justice by members of the slain one's family, is a mandate for the state to punish the murderer. It is quite true that the state is not directly in view in this command, but it is not difficult to see that it is implied and that the historical development from clan to civilized society would carry with it a development of the "seed" mandate from individuals to cooperation of individuals in the more developed civil government. The simple responsibility of indi-

---

6. C. F. Keil and Franz Delitzsch, *Biblical Commentary on the Old Testament, The Pentateuch.* trans. James Martin (Grand Rapids: Eerdmans, n.d.), 1:153.

viduals was superseded by human government itself. This fact is confirmed by the establishment of cities of refuge by Moses, a measure to curb excesses and injustices of the practice of the avenger of blood (Num. 35:9-11). When the time came that the children of Israel had established themselves in Canaan, the greater need for firmer restraint was met through civil authority.

Furthermore, the fact that the punishment was to be exacted because of the "image of God" is evidence that in the light of such priority on human life, the infliction of the punishment was not to be left solely to the whim of individuals but belonged to those who were conscious of the authority given them by God.

Admittedly, the responsibility of the avenger of blood is to be traced to Genesis 9:6. Though the custom is not necessarily explicit from the words "Whoever sheds man's blood, By man his blood shall be shed," it is certainly implied. A fully developed system of law and order with law-enforcement agencies and courts was to come much later than the time of Noah, and, in fact, a system in which the murderer or supposed murderer was brought before others who decided his case did not occur until Israel was settled in Canaan. Even here, though, the responsibility for seeing that justice was done still lay in the hands of the avenger of blood or nearest relative of the slain person.

The law of the avenger of blood was to include, according to Genesis 9:5, the killing of an animal that had killed a man. Later, however, the payment of a ransom by its owner was permitted in Exodus 21:28-36. When the cities of refuge were established, a clear distinction was made between accidental and deliberate murder. In both cases, the murderer could seek asylum at the altar of the sanctuary. If an investigation revealed deliberate murder, he was put to death (Ex. 21:12-17; 1 Kings 1:50; 2:28). The congregation had judgment over the murderer, and they were limited by the regulations of Numbers 35:9-15.

This power of life and death in the hands of men,

therefore, is believed by many to be the necessary foundation of human government in all of its fuller aspects. From this simple mandate, history has witnessed the development of the concept of dealing with insurrection against the state by capital punishment. In other words, it is argued, if the state has not the right to resist those who would defy its laws to the death, then it fails before those who would so dare. Coercive force to the point of the death penalty, whether invoked by the officer of the law who occasionally must take the life of a criminal, or invoked by the executioner who must obey the law of capital punishment of the apprehended murderer, is viewed as absolutely necessary to the state.

It is beyond the scope of this book to delve into this matter, but it is appropriate to note that such delegation of power is recognized by many respected Bible commentators. Luther said of Genesis 9:6:

> Here we have the source from which stem all civil law and the law of nations. If God grants to man power over life and death, surely He also grants power over what is less, such as property, the home, wife, children, servants, and fields. All these God wants to be subject to the power of certain human beings, in order that they may punish the guilty. . . . If God had not conferred this divine power on men, what sort of life do you suppose we would be living? Because He foresaw that there would always be a great abundance of evil men, He established this outward remedy . . . in order that wantoness might not increase beyond measure. With this hedge, these walls, God has given protection for our life and possessions.[7]

Calvin agreed:

> Truly I do not deny that the punishment which the laws ordain   are founded on this divine sentence; but I say

7 Martin Luther, "Against the Robbing and Murdering Peasants," in *The Works of Martin Luther* (Philadelphia: Muhlenberg, 1931), 2.140-41

the words are more comprehensive. It is written, "Men of blood shall not live out half their days" (Ps. lv. 25), and we see some die in highways, some in stews, and many in wars. Therefore, however magistrates may connive at the crime, God sends executioners from many quarters who shall render unto sanguinary men their reward. God so threatens and denounces vengeance against the murderer that he even arms the magistrate with the sword for the avenging of slaughter in order that the blood of men may not be shed with impunity.[8]

COMMAND OR PERMISSION?

Before leaving the mandate of Genesis 9:6, one final question should be considered: Is this a divine command under which God holds man responsible for its execution, or is it a kind of divine permission granted to man should it be required under the demands of some situation? Such a question is more than a fine distinction; it is fundamental. The question involves whether man is here regarded as a bona fide servant of God who has been delegated an awesome responsibility that may be ignored only to the hazard of his blessing from God, or whether he is given merely a tool to use only if he has to. Is the mandate simply a tool placed in man's hands for his own advantage? Or is there involved a moral responsibility? To a large extent, this question is involved in the subject of the purpose of human government and the question of justice, which will receive due attention later.

The context and later revelation strengthen the conviction that Genesis 9:6 is to be understood as a command. First, Genesis 9:5 is to be regarded as God's requiring retribution "at the hand of" every beast and man. This clearly is a *demand* for punishment of every murder, and it refers to the requiring of a proportionate punishment.

8. John Calvin, *Commentaries on the First Book of Moses Called Genesis,* trans. John King (Grand Rapids: Eerdmans, 1948), 1:295.

Second, there is a requirement in the language of verse 6 where the reason for the death penalty is stated to be the fact that man was made in the "image of God." The violation or destruction of that image cannot go unpunished, therefore the murderer's blood must be required. Third, later provisions in the Pentateuch require that the murderer be put to death. Such is the implication of the words "Moreover, you shall not take ransom for the life of a murderer, who is guilty of death" (Num. 35:31).

A command, however, is not without its logical and reasonable exceptions. Accidental homicide, for example, would be one exception. The command, essentially, is to administer justice in regard to a particular crime.

5
The Mandate in
the Mosaic Law

The law regarding capital punishment, stated first in Exodus 21:12, is so explicit and clear that no one is able to contest its meaning. "He who strikes a man so that he dies shall surely be put to death." The mandate has been denied in Genesis 9:6, and it has been denied elsewhere; but there is no question in anyone's mind that Israel was commanded in the Mosaic law to punish the murderer with the death penalty. What is to be found here is not only interpretation of the earlier mandate but an extension of that mandate into other areas.

BASIS OF THE MOSAIC MANDATE

It is safe to say that the Mosaic regulations regarding the death penalty had their basis in the general principle of Genesis 9:6. The Mosaic legislation often had the effect of tempering and controlling practices that, though acceptable in principle, had been abused in actual practice. A notable example of this is found in Mark 10:5 where Jesus gives His law of divorce. He says that Moses' legislation was designed to limit and control a practice that had become excessive, by requiring that a man show reasonable cause for divorcing his wife, the implication of the bill of divorce. Jesus' remark in Mark 10:6 indicates that the original institution of marriage was indissoluble. Thus, the Mosaic law was not necessarily an advance over the original institution but a temporary ethic imposed to control a practice that had got out of hand.

The law of Moses also had this purpose in regard to the practice of capital punishment. The custom of the avenger of blood, a practice which was necessary in the carrying out of the simple and broad mandate of Genesis 9:6 in early society, had probably become excessive, and the spiritual control implied by the reference to the sanctity of life in the words "image of God" had come to be ignored.

At any rate, there is certainly no impression to be received from the Mosaic law that the death penalty was something new. This alone argues for the fact of a mandate in Genesis 9:6. Mosaic legislation is a tacit recognition of a previous mandate.

EXTENSION OF THE MOSAIC MANDATE

In addition to placing necessary restraints upon the practice of the avenger of blood, the Mosaic mandate is conspicuous for the addition of a number of capital offenses. The following list includes offenses besides premeditated murder (Ex. 21:12; Lev. 24:17), and where the manner of execution is mentioned, such is indicated also. Otherwise, there is no prescription of the mode of execution in the text of Scripture, and the nature of it would have to be conjecture:

1. Forms of homicide—child-sacrifice (Lev. 20:2, by stoning); manslaughter, if avenger caught slayer out-

side of city of refuge (Num. 35:27); keeping an ox known to be dangerous, if the ox killed a human being (Ex. 21:29)

2. Bearing false witness on a capital charge (Deut. 18:18-21)
3. Kidnapping (Ex. 21:16)
4. Insult or injury to parents (Ex. 21:15, 17; Lev. 20:9; Deut. 21:18-21, by stoning)
5. Forms of sexual immorality—incest (Lev. 20:14, by burning); unchastity (Deut. 22:21, 24, by stoning); adultery or unnatural vices (Lev. 20:10-16); fornication on the part of a priest's daughter (Lev. 21:9, by burning); fornication on part of a betrothed woman (Gen. 38:24, burning, and Deut. 22: 22-27, by stoning)
6. Various religious offenses—witchcraft, magic, and so on (Ex. 22:18; Lev. 20:6, 27, by stoning); false claim to be a prophet (Deut. 13:5, 10, by stoning); intrusion of alien into sacred place or office (Num. 1:51; 3:10, 38; 18:7); Sabbath-breaking (Ex. 31:14)

PURPOSE OF THE MOSAIC EXTENSION

A close scrutiny of the list of capital offenses reveals a mandate that entered into the civil, moral, and religious realms. Such controls were evidently considered to be expedient for the maintenance of law and order and religious purity as well. A consideration of the degradation of Israel's neighboring nations helps one to understand the severity of these measures, intended to keep her undefiled by Canaanite practices.

Another purpose for such a multiplicity of capital offenses may be suggested in Paul's remark in Galatians 3:24: "Therefore the Law has become our tutor to lead us to Christ, that we may be justified by faith." The law had a pedagogical facet in reference to salvation. Though not given as a way of salvation (Gal. 2:16), the law, nevertheless, has the genius of making a man aware of his need for salvation by grace through faith, in that it presents the standard and holiness of God to which he cannot attain through his own efforts toward righteousness. In other words, the seriousness of sin is often indicated by the punishments prescribed and by the meticulous nature of offerings and sacrifices set forth in the ceremonial sections of the law. The attitude toward leprosy in Leviticus 13 and 14, where it is regarded as a type of sin (cf. Rom. 6:12-14), is another example of the pedagogical nature of law. In the case of adultery and religious impurity, what clearer indication of their seriousness in the sight of God could there be than making them capital offenses? Such a measure certainly taught that in the sight of God there is really no gradation in terms of the seriousness of one sin and another. Perhaps human law, then, when it is functioning as it should, reflects more of justice from the human standpoint, but this justice must be guided by the expressions of absolute justice found in revelation, and this should be tempered with mercy.

Practice of the Mosaic Mandate

It should be of little consequence to the fact of the mandate whether or not the death penalty was faithfully and judiciously carried out as intended. During the early history covered by the Pentateuch and Joshua and Judges, it appears that the administration of the law in capital cases was fairly consistent. In later history, the safeguards built up around the death penalty served practically to nullify its use.

David, who committed the capital crimes of murder and adultery, is often referred to by abolitionists as an example in which the law gave way to a better spirit of mercy, a spirit that is more consistent with the gospel dispensation. Several things, however, must be noted regarding this particular incident that place it into a unique category.

First, Scripture makes clear that David's case was an exception to the rule. Second Samuel 12:13 reads, "Then David said to Nathan, 'I have sinned against the LORD.' And Nathan said to David, 'The LORD also has taken away your sin; you shall not die.' " Such language certainly indicates that David recognized that death would have been just and deserved. There is a serious question of whether civil law provided for the enforcement of the statute in the case of an absolute king. At any rate, if this were the case, God would have been capable of seeing that justice was done, but such was not the purpose of God; that is, to take David's life as a direct result of this sin (2 Sam. 12:10-11). It is no threat to the rightness of capital punishment to find exceptions to the rule in Scripture. The recognition of such exceptions is merely an indication of the fact that murder is not always dealt with by God's taking the murderer's life.

Second, David was divinely forgiven, a prerogative that God may exercise. That such a prerogative could not belong to the state is seen in the fact that this forgiveness was announced by a divinely accredited prophet, Nathan. This divine forgiveness could be applied because God could judge the sincerity of David's repentance, an ability that does not belong to finite man.

There is one final question about the practice of the Mosaic mandate for today. Can such an ancient document as the law of Moses be implemented in the twentieth century? Part of the answer lies in the fact that modern practice need not be considered as an implementation of Mosaic law necessarily, but rather the Noahic mandate.

Earlier it was noted that Charles Colson had grave doubts that Mosaic law could be considered the basis for any modern practice on two counts: (1) *two* witnesses were required for passing the death penalty; and (2) the witnesses were the first to cast the stones; that is, they participated in the executions. Is it consistent to advocate capital punishment without all the rules by which Scripture surrounded it?

One could insist that the original Genesis 9:6 mandate gave no details for enforcement, and that the state is at liberty to make its own rules, thus sidestepping the Mosaic law altogether. However, there is probably a better approach than this, one that will enable us to take seriously the Word of God as it appears in the Mosaic legislation and to benefit from some of its insights..

This approach is to recognize that in much of Scripture our interpretation requires us to seek for enduring principles by recognizing the historical and cultural elements that are not normative and sifting out the lasting principles. The question in the case of the death penalty in the Mosaic law is: Are the requirements pertaining to the witnesses a matter of culture, or do they stand as timeless principles? In my judgment, contained in them are two principles, so that the application in a literal manner cannot be insisted upon. These principles are (1) the evidence against the defendent must be *convincing* (the requirement for two witnesses), and (2) the witnesses should themselves be *fully truthful* and *responsible,* as shown by their willingness to participate in the execution.[1]

Are these principles carried out in some equivalent way in modern jurisprudence? Probably so. The kind of evidence, though often circumstantial, must leave the jury without a shadow of doubt of the defendant's guilt. As to responsibility, witnesses are subject to penalties for perjury and swear to tell the whole truth as they give their testimony. In ancient times two witnesses were necessary because societies lacked the crime detection apparatus that is available today. Since stoning is not a form of punishment anymore, there is not available this rather convenient way to achieve responsible testimony by participation.

The New Testament still commands the honoring of

---

1. See C. F. Keil and Franz Delitzsch, *The Pentateuch* (reprint, Grand Rapids: Eerdmans, 1978), p. 381.

mothers and fathers even though by that time incorrigible children were not stoned to death.

QUESTION OF THE SIXTH COMMANDMENT

The sixth commandment, "Thou shalt not kill" (Ex. 20:13, King James Version), is frequently quoted as an argument against capital punishment. If the word translated "kill" includes all forms of life-taking, it poses a serious contradiction to the mandate that has been discussed.

MEANING OF THE SIXTH COMMANDMENT

The sixth commandment covers, in addition to acts of violence or stratagem, every act that endangers human life, whether it arises from carelessness (Deut. 22:8), wantonness (Lev. 19:14), or hatred, anger, and revenge (Lev. 19:17-18). Furthermore, since the sixth commandment is the first commandment of the second table, involving man's duty to his fellow man, life is placed at the head as the basis of human existence and the depository of the human personality, which is the image of God. The absence of an object of the killing is a clear indication that the commandment includes the destruction of one's own life.

John Calvin, in his classic comments on the Ten Commandments in the *Institutes of the Christian Religion,* approaches the sixth commandment from a positive standpoint, from the standpoint of its purpose, which purpose is that "each man ought to concern himself with the safety of all."[2] Calvin also calls attention to the fact that Christ made so clear in Matthew 5:22, that murder

2. John Calvin, *Institutes of the Christian Religion,* ed. John T. McNeill, trans. Ford L. Battles (Philadelphia: Westminster, 1965), 1:404.

involves the heart "and enjoins the inner intent to save a brother's life."[3]

The word *radzah* means to dash in pieces or to kill, especially with premeditation.[4] Actually, Hebrew has no word for murder. Both the nominal forms, *meradzeah,* "manslayer," and *rodzeah,* "homicide," can apply to premeditated, malicious killing and accidental killing. In Numbers 35:19 *radzah* is used in connection with the avenger of blood as well as for the manslayer, but the act of the avenger of blood is specifically exempt for "blood-guiltiness," that is, from the penalty of murder (Num. 35:27).

The word *radzah* appears forty-nine times in the Old Testament. Of these, thirty-six are in the Pentateuch and Joshua, all of which relate to laws regarding murder and manslaughter. Of the remaining thirteen occurrences, two (Ezek. 21:22 and Ps. 42:10) involve the nominal form in an abstract use and are thus not relevant. Two more (Jer. 7:9 and Hos. 4:2) are quotations of the sixth commandment and cannot have any bearing on the use of the word (the NASB translates Jer. 7:9 as "murder"). In Psalm 62:3 nothing can be proved either way. In Proverbs 22:24 it should be translated "murdered" in order to preserve its meaning. In the seven remaining cases outside of the Mosaic code, every one clearly means murder (Judg. 20:4; 1 Kings 21:19; 2 Kings 6:32; Job 24:14; Ps. 94:6; Isa. 1:21; Hos. 6:9). *Radzah* is never used of animals, God, angels, or of enemies in battle.

In the Greek Septuagint version of the Old Testament, the Greek *phoneutes,* "murder," is used to translate *radzah* sixteen times and never for any other word. *Phoneuo*

---

3. Ibid.
4. *Gesenius' Hebrew and Chaldee Lexicon,* trans. S. P. Tregelles (Grand Rapids: Eerdmans, 1954), pp. 778-79, and *International Standard Bible Encyclopedia,* s.v. "Murder," both confirm the important usage of this word in connection with premeditation.

is used for *radzah* twenty-nine or thirty times and only nine or ten times for all other words put together. In the New Testament, the sixth commandment is always translated by *phoneuo,* which is never employed in any other sense than "to murder."[5]

On the basis of its common usage, therefore, the Hebrew word in the sixth commandment must be translated "murder."

RELEVANCE OF THE SIXTH COMMANDMENT

The sixth commandment has in view violent, willful, and malicious assault upon human life, and that is indicated by at least two other factors in addition to the meaning of the word *radzah.* First, the penalty for breaking the commandment is stated in Exodus 21:12, and it is death.[6] The same penalty is stated in Numbers 35:16-21. Consequently, the state that takes the life of the murderer is not guilty of the crime forbidden in the commandment that forbids murder. Therefore, any argument against capital punishment on the basis of the sixth commandment ignores the meaning of the word and the context as well. Strictly speaking, the Ten Commandments are given as standards for personal conduct, and therefore no application can be made to execution by duly constituted civil authorities operating under the divine mandate. Jesus kept murder in the realm of personal conduct when He identified it with hate (Matt. 5:21-22).

---

5. William F. Arndt and F. Wilbur Gingrich, *A Greek-English Lexicon of the New Testament* (Chicago: U. of Chicago, 1957), p. 872; J. H. Moulton and G. Milligan, *The Vocabulary of the Greek Testament* (Grand Rapids: Eerdmans, 1949), p. 674.
6. Since all Ten Commandments had the death penalty attached to them, one might argue that it is inconsistent to attempt to retain the death penalty for one commandment and not all the rest as well. This argument would fail to account for the fact that one need not go to Ex. 21:12 to find his basis for capital punishment, for that text was Israel's mandate.

Second, the fact that the sixth commandment refers to premeditated murder is demonstrated by the later provision for cities of refuge (Num. 35), where the manslayer could seek asylum for an accidental or justified slaying.

It is important to remember that God commanded Israel to put her enemies to death during the conquest of Canaan. Here divine punishment was being executed at the hands of God's chosen people. The sixth commandment obviously did not pertain to that sort of killing.

Conclusion

On the basis of the meaning of the Hebrew word translated "kill" and the death penalty attached to the violation of the sixth commandment, it must be concluded that the sixth commandment is irrelevant to the issue of capital punishment. Furthermore, the mandate of the Mosaic law is clear. It is not threatened by the failure on the part of its subjects to apply it. This mandate had its more immediate purpose in controlling the evil tendencies of individuals and placing a moral hedge about the people of Israel. It had its more remote purpose in teaching man something of the nature and consequences of sin and thus pointing him eventually to Jesus Christ the Savior.

6
The Teaching of Jesus

Those who recognize the authority of Scripture generally recognize that the New Testament has the last word on any subject. This idea will be developed later in relation to the charges by abolitionists that such things as the death of Christ and the abolition of the law of Moses have served to abolish capital punishment. However, at this point we shall consider passages in the New Testament that may have some bearing on the validity of capital punishment for today. If capital punishment is recognized as a valid institution in the New Testament, then it is a valid institution today.

It is not suggested that Jesus offered any civil legislation for this age, however. That was not His purpose. His message was primarily a redemptive one, and even in the Sermon on the Mount, which represents the "constitution," so to speak, of the kingdom of heaven, His legislation is on the personal level.

It must also be recognized that a good deal of Jesus' teaching was given during a time of transition. This fact probably affects minor details more than major teachings, for most of the teaching of the epistles was given by way of exposition of teachings of Christ. Nevertheless, when Jesus touched upon elements of the Mosaic system that had been misinterpreted or misused, He made that fact quite clear, the most notable being the Pharisees' teaching on personal vengeance. Surely, if capital punishment had been misapplied He would have said something to that effect.

The point of this chapter is that, though the evidence is not always unambiguous in favor of capital punishment, neither did Jesus clearly reject it, and that a careful examination of the details of several passages points to the probability that He tacitly assumed the mandate of Genesis 9:6.

MATTHEW 5:21-22

In Matthew 5:21-22, a portion of the Sermon on the Mount, the issue is not whether Jesus offered explicit teaching on capital punishment but whether He may have been assuming its validity in passing. The passage is as follows:

> You have heard that the ancients were told, "You shall not commit murder" and "Whoever commits murder shall be liable to the court." But I say to you that everyone who is angry with his brother shall be guilty before the court; and whoever shall say to his brother, "Raca," shall be guilty before the supreme court; and whoever shall say, "You fool," shall be guilty enough to go into the fiery hell.

Jesus began His exposition by first quoting the law of Exodus 20:13, "You shall not commit murder," and then including as part of His quotation the scribal gloss, "Whoever commits murder," and so forth. The scribal addition implied that the sum total of the law rested in the outward act only, the impact of the reference to coming into judgment. Jesus' purpose was to strip away the tendency to mere external obedience and carry the law on further to apply also to the attitudes of the inner man, which He did in verse 22 where He says that a man is in danger of the judgment even if he so much as becomes angry with his brother.

In doing this, though, Jesus placed His approval on the practice that was implied by the word "court," or "judgment" (Gk, *krisis*). There are two possible meanings for this term: the judgment prescribed in Exodus 21:12-15, which was the death penalty, or the local council of elders in each city.[1]

When Jesus moved on to the idea of hate toward one's brother, which He made as serious as murder, He used another term, "council" (Gk, *Sanhedrin*), probably as a synonym for what was implied when He used "judgment." In other words, anger is as serious as murder, and punishment will be carried out by the Council, which is the Supreme Court of the land. Since the Sanhedrin were vested with the responsibility of recommending the death penalty, the force of Jesus' remark is an approval of such a practice.[2]

Since Jesus was unhesitatingly changing or revising much of what their tradition prescribed, it is gratuitous to object that a mere reference to a practice is not an approval. Besides, what Jesus said about the dangers of hell for showing contempt to a brother loses much force if what He said referred to something of which He disapproved. What He meant is, if murder gets you the death penalty, even hatred and contempt get you worse—eter-

---

1. See Alan H. McNeile, *The Gospel According to Matthew* (reprint, Grand Rapids: Baker, 1980), p. 61, for the death penalty; and Robert Gundry, *Matthew: A Commentary on His Literary and Theological Art* (Grand Rapids: Eerdmans, 1982), p. 85, for the local court.
2. See Josephus, *Antiquities of the Jews,* trans. William Whiston, 4.8.14.

nal punishment—because they are the root of it all.

In Matthew 5:38 and 39 Jesus makes clear that the *lex talionis* does not apply to one's personal code, that one should not seek personal revenge in attacks upon himself, but this does not necessarily abolish the *lex talionis* as a valid principle of justice in civil matters as the case seems to be when He discusses the judgment for murder.

It may be further significant that in His reference to adultery (Matt. 5:27-28), He omits any mention of the Mosaic punishment, which was also the death penalty. This may harmonize, though such an assumption is precarious, with His action regarding the woman taken in adultery in John 8. Could we speculate that Christ was abolishing the death penalty for adultery but not for murder? If that was the case, He would merely be returning to Genesis as the primary mandate, because that pertained only to murder.

MATTHEW 26:50-52

Matthew 26:50-52 has been quoted merely to justify pacifism. Such an interpetation may not do justice to the context in which it appears:

> Then they came and laid hands on Jesus and seized Him. And behold, one of those who were with Jesus reached and drew out his sword, and struck the slave of the high priest, and cut off his ear. Then Jesus said to him, "Put your sword back into its place; for all those who take up the sword shall perish by the sword."

Not realizing yet the significance of Jesus' submission to the authorities in order that He might be crucified, Peter attempted to take things into his own hands and resisted arrest by the authorities. What Peter did was not only a violation of the spiritual purposes of Christ's submission, but also an act that violated a civil code and that was punishable by death.

The question is, how much can be drawn out of the words "All those who take up the sword shall perish by the sword"? Commentator John Peter Lange saw this statement as a "judicial sentence" that rested upon an absolutely universal principle. He described this principle in the following words.

> The sword is visited by the sword in war; the sword of retribution opposes the arbitrary sword of rebellious sedition; and the sword taken up unspiritually in a spiritual cause, is avenged by the certain, though perhaps long delayed, sword of historical vengeance. . . . Peter had really forfeited his life to the sword; but the Lord rectified his wounded position by the correcting word which He spoke, by the miraculous healing of the ear. . . . Therefore, the Lord so solemnly denounced his act, pronounced an ideal sentence of death upon his head, which, however, was graciously repealed.[3]

Instead of Jesus' words being a statement about the morality of war, they pertain to a civil violation. Another authority, Henry Alford, goes so far as to say that the verse is "a repetition . . . of Gen. ix, 6. This should," he continues, "be thought of by those well-meaning but shallow persons who seek to abolish the punishment of death in Christian states.[4]

Those older interpreters are joined in their exegesis by several modern ones. Lenski, for example, sees Jesus *disavowing* Peter's act by affirming the illegality of what he was doing.[5] Tasker notes that this verse cannot pertain to pacifism because of the context and the simple fact

3. John Peter Lange, "The Gospel According to Matthew," in *Lange's Commentary on the Holy Scriptures* (Grand Rapids: Zondervan, n.d.), p. 486.
4. Henry Alford, *The Greek Testament* (Boston: Lee & Shepard, 1886), 1:273-79.
5. R. C. H. Lenski, *The Interpretation of St. Matthew's Gospel* (Minneapolis: Augsburg, 1943), pp. 1051-52.

that it is not true that all who take the sword in war die by the sword.[6]

Many agree that what Jesus said about the sword was actually a current proverb taken from a Jewish commentary ("targum") on Isaiah 50:11. If this is so, a pacifistic interpretation is a bit foreign to first-century thinking about war.

These considerations serve, then, to make the words of Jesus quite plausibly pertain to the law of retribution, and thus to the question of capital punishment.

JOHN 8:1-11

Though most textual scholars believe John 8:1-11 was not originally a part of the gospel of John, since it is missing in the oldest Greek manuscripts, most nevertheless accept it as an authentic record of an actual incident in the life of Christ. It reads as follows:

> . . . Jesus went to the Mount of Olives. And early in the morning He came again into the temple, and all the people were coming to Him; and He sat down and began to teach them. And the scribes and the Pharisees brought a woman caught in adultery, and having set her in the midst, they said to Him, "Teacher, this woman has been caught in adultery, in the very act. Now in the Law Moses commanded us to stone such women; what then do You say?" And they were saying this, testing Him, in order that they might have grounds for accusing Him. But Jesus stooped down, and with His finger wrote on the ground. But when they persisted in asking Him, He straightened up, and said to them, "He who is without sin among you, let him be the first to throw a stone at her." And again He stooped down, and wrote on the ground. And when they heard it, they began to go out one by one, beginning with the older

6 R. V. G. Tasker, *The Gospel According to St. Matthew* (Grand Rapids: Eerdmans, 1961), p. 251.

ones, and He was left alone, and the woman, where she had been, in the midst. And straightening up, Jesus said to her, "Woman where are they? Did no one condemn you?" And she said, "No one, Lord." And Jesus said, "Neither do I condemn you; go your way. From now on sin no more."

Two factors severely limit the importance of this text in the discussion of capital punishment, the textual problem already mentioned and the uncertainty to the implications of Jesus' words "Neither do I condemn you." Mainly because the passage has been used to prove that Jesus did not require the death penalty, an alternative interpretation is offered here.

Some abolitionists of the death penalty insist that Jesus made a judicial ruling on capital punishment when He refused to require the death penalty for an offense that the Mosaic law punished with death. For example, John H. Yoder says:

> When Jesus Himself was asked to rule on an offense which by the laws of the time called for the death penalty, His answer was clearly such as to abolish it; not directly by declaring it a wrong institution, but indirectly by demanding that the judges and executioners must first be sinless.[7]

Does such a view square with Jesus' initial silence in the matter? The first question that must be asked is, Were the Pharisees asking for His judgment or His *opinion?* Were they asking Him to sit in the place of a civil magistrate, or were they consulting Him, as it were, for His legal advice? F. F. Bruce offers the following explanation:

> Both questions were calculated to impale Jesus on the horns of a dilemma: if he answered one way, he would forfeit popular good will; if he answered the other way, he

---

7. John Howard Yoder, *The Christian and Capital Punishment* (Newton, Kan.: Faith & Life, 1961), p. 4.

could be charged with sedition before the Roman governor. If he gave an independent ruling on the point of issue, and especially if he said that the death penalty should be carried out, he could be accused of usurping the governor's jurisdiction, or of usurping jurisdiction which the Roman administration had expressly reserved to the Sanhedrin. The Sanhedrin retained the right to *pronounce* the death sentence for capital offences against Jewish law, although they could not *execute* it without the governor's authorization (see 18:31). These were matters with which a layman would be well advised not to meddle; but Jesus was now challenged to speak his mind on such a matter.[8]

Jesus was not qualified, so far as they were probably concerned, to render such a civil verdict, because He was not a duly authorized judge. He was not a member of the Sanhedrin. To judge would have been contrary to Jesus' purpose and mission. He stated clearly (John 12:47) that His mission at that time was not to judge but to save the world. Could this better explain His silence before them?

The second question is, What was the exact nature of Jesus' response when He was pressed for an answer? The text is as follows: "But when they persisted in asking Him, He straightened up, and said to them, 'He who is without sin among you, let him be the first to throw a stone at her.' " Yoder argues that when a case involving capital punishment was brought to Jesus, He merely required that a "qualified executioner" step forward—one who himself was perfect and free from sin. In the absence of such a person, therefore, Jesus was in effect saying that no qualified executioner *exists* in capital cases. This is reading a lot into the passage that simply is not there, though Jesus was apparently calling in ques-

---

8. F. F. Bruce, *The Gospel of John* (Grand Rapids: Eerdmans, 1983), p. 415.

tion the moral qualifications of those gathered to seek His opinion. How can this call into question the validity of the law itself? Was He not saying instead, "All right, I recognize the demands of the law. Assuming that this woman is actually guilty, would it not be appropriate, in the light of the seriousness of her crime, to allow the one who is righteous among you to cast the first stone?" Of course, another possibility is that Jesus was not asking for a sinless person to cast the first stone but merely one who was not himself an adulterer like the woman.

Those who would argue for abolition of the death penalty on the basis of the moral qualifications of the executioner, or the judge or jury for that matter, would, in order to be consistent, rule out the ability of human courts to render a verdict on anything. Why draw a moral distinction for capital cases only? More is to be said for the argument from human fallibility in terms of deciding the guilt or innocence of the accused than this argument, at least as far as capital cases are concerned. Furthermore, this argument assumes that Jesus challenged the right of execution of *all* the potential executioners. Actually, He merely suggested that the *first* one to cast a stone be without sin. Hypothetically, in other words, everyone else was welcome to join the execution once this sinless individual had cast his stone. In point of fact, Jesus Himself was not questioning their right to take the woman's life, but He was simply using an ingenius device to prevent them from doing so at His advice. His words "He who is without sin among you, let him be the first to throw a stone at her" could be construed to be a recognition of the mandate, but it may be only the mandate of the Mosaic law, which would not be convincing to those who regard that law to be totally abolished.

Finally, this incident involves a case of adultery, not murder. Perhaps the most that can be said about the whole issue is that Jesus, acting in harmony with the Matthew 5 passage on adultery, simply sets aside the death penalty for adultery, not necessarily the death penalty for murder.

JOHN 19:10-11

In His crucifixion, Jesus encountered the power of civil government. Jesus' attitude toward that power, especially the power of life and death, may be pertinent to the issue if it appears anywhere. Though He submitted to that government, would it not seem natural for Him to have condemned what they were doing had they acted from an assumption of power that really was not theirs? There appears in John 19:11 a possible recognition of the divine right of government to pass the death penalty. In this passage Jesus confirms Pilate's claim to have "power" (NASB, "authority") over Him:

> Pilate therefore said to Him, "You do not speak to me? Do You not know that I have authority to release You, and I have authority to crucify You?" Jesus answered, "You would have no authority over Me, unless it had been given you from above; for this reason he who delivered Me up to you has the greater sin."

THE NATURE OF PILATE'S POWER

Some have superficially assumed that Jesus here refers to the plan of God, which has brought Pilate, an unwitting instrument, into such a place as this in order to see to the crucifixion of Christ. This, however, would appear to implicate God Himself in the crucifixion as its primary cause, because it would seem to rule out Pilate's free choice in making the decision. God is sovereign, of course, and all evil choices are part of His eternal decree by way of *permission*. Nevertheless, to say that God had "authorized" Pilate's right to crucify Jesus Christ is saying much more than sovereign permission.

The word translated "authority" (Gk, *exousia*) better expresses an idea of mandated authority by an accredited ruler, as it indeed does in Romans 13 where the "governing authorities" are to be obeyed unquestioningly. The idea of permitted but not legal *control* over Jesus would have been better expressed by another word like the Greek *kratos.*

It is more consistent to recognize here an authority, or power, granted by the directive will of God, the authority vested in all human government to execute the death penalty. After all, Pilate's reference was to his specific authority to pass the death sentence, not to some vague power over Jesus Himself. The additional sentence, "for this reason he who delivered Me up to you has the greater sin," tends to confirm this interpretation. The high priest was acting under God's "permission"; why would he be under greater condemnation that Pilate? The point must be that Pilate at least stood partly on firm ground: the mandate of God. Though he allowed this mandate to be perverted, thus incurring guilt to himself, he at least did not act totally apart from legal warrant.

John Calvin agrees that this passage does not refer to the general permission of God but to the "office of the Magistrate."[9] Karl Barth also sees here a recognition of the mandate of the state.[10] C. K. Barrett says: "All human authority is derived from God's. . . . It is implied primarily that in condemning and crucifying Jesus, Pilate acts with divine consent."[11] Frederick Godet adds in a similar vein: "Pilate speaks only of his power; Jesus reminds him of his dependence and responsibility."[12] Comparing this passage to Romans 13, Westcott says:

9. John Calvin, *Commentary on the Gospel According to John,* trans. William Pringle (Grand Rapids: Eerdmans, 1949), 2:221.
10. Karl Barth, *Community, State, and Church, Three Essays* (Garden City: Anchor, 1960), p. 110.
11. C. K. Barrett, *The Gospel According to St. John* (London: SPCK, 1955), p. 452.
12. Frederick Godet, *Commentary on the Gospel of John* (Edinburgh: T. & T. Clark, 1893), 3:259.

In the order of the world Pilate had the authority which he claimed to have. It had been given to him to exercise authority. As the representative of the Emperor his judgment was legally decisive (Rom. xiii. 1). But still his right to exercise authority was derived, not inherent. Human government is only valid as the expression of the divine will. He therefore who exercises it is responsible . . . to a higher power.[13]

To summarize, John 19:11 very possibly shows Jesus' recognition of the mandate that Pilate possessed as the representative of an earthly government. Pilate's own reference to the right of capital punishment serves to strengthen the idea that Jesus' remark, though possibly referring to a broader authority vested in the state, pertained specifically to the mandate of the death penalty. At any rate, Jesus did not challenge that right, though this would have been the most appropriate place to have done so.

Finally, this passage is significant in the sense that a Gentile power is involved. No one can claim that the Mosaic mandate, which had passed from the scene along with its clear right to punish with the death sentence, is involved here. In addition, no hint was made by Christ that this mandate was about to be repealed in any manner by His death. His sacrifice was to redeem individual men through their personal faith, not necessarily the state as well.

THE MISUSE OF POWER

Though Pilate had the authority of which he spoke, he certainly failed to use it properly. Abolitionists of the death penalty have often referred to the crucifixion as a classic example of why men should not be put to death by the state. From the standpoint of liberal theology,

13 B F Westcott, *The Gospel According to St. John* (Grand Rapids: Eerdmans, 1951), p 302

which views the death of Christ as merely an unfortunate martyrdom, this argument is no surprise. But it is surprising to find evangelicals arguing this way. Certainly Jesus' death involved a miscarriage of justice, a misuse of power, but does this fact deny that the power exists rightfully?

The fact of this misuse was recognized by Jesus Himself in His remark about who had the greater guilt (John 19:11*b*). It was the high priest and the Jewish leaders who involved legitimate government in their own lawless desires.

Important also is the fact that technically Jesus was not condemned by Pilate as guilty of His alleged crime. Pilate pronounced Him a "just man" (Matt. 27:19-24; Mark 15:14; Luke 23:14-15, 22; John 18:38; 19:4, 6) and sought to release Him at first. Jesus, however, was crucified *in spite* of what Pilate had to say to the issue, not in accordance with it. But the fact that Pilate allowed a miscarriage of justice to take place does not alter the fact that his authority was given to him from above.

For the sake of accuracy, we should observe that Jesus' recognition of the mandate in John 19:11 actually goes beyond the issue of the death penalty for premeditated murder and extends to the death penalty for insurrection against the state, assuming the validity of my interpretation. Rather than limit the death penalty to that particular crime, however, Jesus' recognition of a mandate should instead be seen as a broader view that encompasses both murder and insurrection, for Pilate had reference to his power to put men to death for either crime, if Roman law is taken into consideration.

7
The Teaching of the Apostles

The apostles are recognized by most scholars as being in harmony with the teaching of Christ. In fact, the epistles are frequently looked upon as being expository in relation to the gospels, and the book of Acts is often regarded as an extension of the ministry of Christ through the apostles. In regard to the subject at hand, such passages as Romans 13, 1 Corinthians 6, and 1 Corinthians 2:8 coincide completely with Jesus' concept of the state.

Several passages in the Acts and epistles touch upon the question of capital punishment. The fact that the New Testament contains relatively little on the subject certainly cannot be regarded as having a material bearing on the subject, for at least two good reasons. First, the apostles were primarily concerned with the spiritual message of the gospel and truth relative to it. Only when this truth touched upon issues involving the state does teaching appear that is relevant to capital punishment. Second, the fact of the mandate and its general purpose had already been clearly established in Genesis 9:6 and in the law of Moses. Only further clarification of this existing mandate and its relation to the new people of God, the church, needed to be made.

Acts 25:11

Acts 25:11, though not appearing with the express purpose of teaching anything about the subject of capital punishment, nevertheless constitutes a clear recognition of the mandate. The passage is as follows:

> But Festus, wishing to do the Jews a favor, answered Paul and said, "Are you willing to go up to Jerusalem and stand trial before me on these charges?" But Paul said, "I am standing before Caesar's tribunal, where I ought to be tried. I have done no wrong to the Jews, as you also very well know. If then I am a wrongdoer, and have committed anything worthy of death, I do not refuse to die; but if none of those things is true of which these men accuse me, no one can hand me over to them. I appeal to Caesar." (Acts 25:9-11)

Opponents of the death penalty have evaded this passage by claiming that Paul was only saying he did not deserve to die, that he was not recognizing the rightness or wrongness of capital punishment.[1] Another evasion is in the claim that Paul merely states he had no intention of being a fugitive from martyrdom.[2]

Such evasions fail to note the fact that Paul would have been hypocritical in making such a statement had he really regarded the Roman government's right to pass the death penalty as morally wrong. Can a reference to "any-

1. Arnold B. Rhodes, et. al., "Bible and Capital Punishment," *Eternity* 8 (June 1961): 21.
2. L. B. Smedes, "Is the Death Penalty Necessary?" *United Evangelical Action* 23 (December 1964): 19.

thing worthy of death" possibly be construed as being a description of a martyrdom? Paul was accused of breaking a law; he was not being tried for his religious convictions, though his convictions were indirectly related.

What is the meaning of Paul's statement in Acts 25:11? It seems clear that Paul recognizes that there are crimes "worthy" of death and that human government to which he would make his appeal had the right to inflict that penalty. F. F. Bruce agrees:

> It was not, he assured Festus, that he wished to circumvent the law of Rome or escape the due reward of anything he might have done. If he had in fact committed a capital crime, as his accusers alleged, he was prepared to suffer the supreme penalty for it, but if there was no substance in their charges, he must be placed in their power. Let Roman justice decide.[3]

He had confidence, indeed, in Roman justice. It is further evidence that Paul approved of Roman justice in the death penalty when he made his appeal to Caesar. This was done in order to prevent a miscarriage of justice that he evidently foresaw, should the Jews' desires be granted and his case be tried in Jerusalem. Would Paul seek Roman justice if he considered that justice wrong in exercising the death penalty? It appears that Paul was referring to more than just taking his chances with Roman justice rather than Jewish justice. As a Roman citizen, he had experienced the benefits of Roman justice before, and his words "anything worthy of death" certainly seem to reflect his general approval of the Roman system of justice. The phrase "worthy of death" might or might not reflect a recognition of the death penalty by

3. F. F. Bruce, "Commentary on the Book of Acts," in *New International Commentary on the New Testament* (Grand Rapids: Eerdmans, 1956), pp. 477-78.

itself, but the context of Paul's appeal invests it with the significance of a moral judgment of the system to which he appeals. He would have avoided the phrase and simply made an appeal for justice in his own case, otherwise. Such language would be unnecessary to his appeal. The recognition of a divine mandate in this incident is contextually sound.

ROMANS 13:1-7

In the context of Romans 13:1-7 the apostle Paul has turned to the practical application of his theological exposition of sin and righteousness. Beginning with Romans 12:9 he gives instructions regarding human relationships which bring him to the question of the Christian's relationship to government in chapter 13. What follows is the classic passage of the New Testament on the Christian view of human government:

> Let every person be in subjection to the governing authorities. For there is no authority except from God, and those which exist are established by God. Therefore . . . they who have opposed will receive condemnation upon themselves. For rulers are not a cause of fear for good behavior, but for evil. Do you want to have no fear of authority? Do what is good, and you will have praise from the same; for it is a minister of God to you for good. But if you do what is evil, be afraid; for it does not bear the sword for nothing; for it is a minister of God, an avenger who brings wrath upon the one who practices evil. Wherefore it is necessary to be in subjection, not only because of wrath, but also for conscience' sake. For because of this you also pay taxes, for rulers are servants of God, devoting themselves to this very thing. Render to all what is due them: tax to whom tax is due; custom to whom custom; fear to whom fear; honor to whom honor. (Rom. 13:1-7)

PAUL'S CONCEPT OF THE STATE

The apostle Paul, in harmony with Jesus' teaching, conceives of the state as a servant with delegated authority. This authority is even so direct that he refers to the civil magistrate as the "minister" of God, a term used also of that spiritual function in the church. But this relationship is not quite the same as that relationship of Jesus Christ to the church that Paul describes in 1 Corinthians 12:12-27 and Ephesians 4:6 as the head to the body. Paul's concept is that the state has a divinely ordained role to fill but that the church is vitally united to Jesus Christ by virtue of the baptism of the Holy Spirit (1 Cor. 12:13).

Some abolitionists attempt to link the authority of the state with the lordship of Christ over all things (Eph. 1:21).[4] They then conveniently find an inconsistency between this lordship and capital punishment. However, the authority of the state does not reside in such a dominion. The lordship over "every principality and power" (Eph. 1:21) is not the lordship over the church; in fact, it is not even called "lordship." It is called "dominion." Ephesians 1:21 speaks of the *subjection* of these powers. *Lordship,* when used of Christ, implies that His subjects recognize the fact (Eph. 4:5). It is more logical to view Paul's concept of the state in terms of a separate mandate for human government.

Paul's idea of the state stands in sharp contrast to that of the church. The context of Romans 13:1-7 bears this out in remarkable fashion. The ethic for the church or individual Christian is stated beginning with Romans 12:9 and continues on up to the beginning of Romans 13. Then this same ethic is continued by way of contrast again beginning with Romans 13:8. In the passage pre-

---

4. John Howard Yoder, *The Christian and Capital Punishment* (Newton, Kan.: Faith & Life, 1961), p. 15.

ceding Romans 13:1-7, the Christian ethic is summed up in such words as these:

> Never pay back evil for evil to anyone. Respect what is right in the sight of all men. If possible, so far as it depends on you, be at peace with all men. Never take your own revenge, beloved, but leave room for the wrath of God, for it is written, "Vengeance is Mine, I will repay," says the Lord. "But if your enemy is hungry, feed him, and if he is thirsty, give him a drink; for in so doing you will heap burning coals upon his head." Do not be overcome by evil, but overcome evil with good. (Rom. 12:17-21)

Following Paul's statement in Romans 13:1-7, beginning with verse 8, the ethic of love for one's neighbor again appears. The command to "owe nothing to any one" (Rom. 13:8), refers, of course, to the dues, taxes, tribute, custom, fear, and honor of Romans 13:7.

The command of Romans 12:19, "Never take your own revenge," refers not to a refusal to seek justice but to an attempt to seek justice in a personal way, for the same word occurs in Romans 13:4, where the civil magistrate is the "avenger," evidently executing the kind of vengeance that Romans 12:19 ascribes to the Lord. Thus the magistrate does so as the "minister of God" (Rom. 13:4). The idea of the magistrate's being the "minister of God" is that of vice-regent, and the expression "avenger for wrath" is an avenger by office to satisfy the demands of wrath.

Though the passages preceding and following Romans 13:1-7 present the Christian ethic in terms of love and forgiveness, there is no indication whatsoever that civil laws should be changed so that leniency is shown to the criminal. Rather, even the Christian himself is warned in Romans 13:3 to "do that which is good," or he places himself under the same wrath as the common law-breaker. The Christian is to live above the law so that he does not come under its judgment.

IMMORAL VERSUS THE MORAL STATE

It is clear that Paul recognizes the divine sanction of the state in Romans 13, but what of the problem of such power in the hands of an "immoral" government; specifically, what about capital punishment in the hands of evil rulers?

First of all, though Paul makes no attempt to deal with this problem in Romans 13, his words "[the powers] which exist are established by God" do not necessarily mean that all powers are moral because their power is ordained by God. Paul probably has in mind government as a principle, not individual governments.

Jesus Himself gives us a general principle that is helpful in our thinking about power in the hands of immoral men: "render to Caesar the things that are Caesar's; and to God the things that are God's" (Matt. 22:21). In other words, "Caesar" (human government) has his own delegated sphere of operation. This sphere is limited, at least to the extent of what rightfully belongs to God. This means that if human government requires that which is contrary to God's will for us, it has stepped beyond its sphere and need no longer be recognized as making legitimate demands in that particular area.

What, then, would be the Christian's proper response under such circumstances? At least one rule of thumb is suggested in Acts 4:19 where the Sanhedrin (who stood, for all practical purposes, in the place of constituted government under the Roman arrangement) forbade the disciples to preach the gospel. Peter answered, "Whether it is right in the sight of God to give heed to you rather than to God, you be the judge; for we cannot stop speaking what we have seen and heard" (Acts 4:19-20). Peter and the disciples disobeyed the command, continued preaching, and suffered the consequences. They did not incite a rebellion. They "passively" resisted; that is, without violence.

Thus, Christians are obligated to recognize the difference between an immoral and a legitimate use of power. They can do this without denying the principle of human government. They are to be "subject" to the "powers that be," and that includes exerting influences upon government to do that which is moral, if possible. It is not the presence of immoral men in government (e.g., Nero ruled when Paul wrote Romans 13) that disqualifies it necessarily. It is the immoral use of power that removes government from the sphere into which God originally placed it.

Capital punishment, by the same token, need not necessarily be condemned as a principle, simply because men like Hitler or Stalin use it to purge those whom they imagine threaten their regime. At any rate, abolition of the death penalty by a legitimate government certainly will never prevent tyrants from using it to gain or preserve their power. Under such circumstances a better label for such power of death would be "murder," not capital punishment.

THE STATE'S RIGHT TO "AVENGE" EVIL

Despite the clear teaching of Paul regarding the right of the magistrate to execute vengeance, there are those who argue that this does not extend to capital punishment. To some, for example, the "sword" represents capital punishment no more than a policeman's pistol. It is a symbol of the right of government to use force if necessary, they say, in the function of the civil magistrate in maintaining law and order.[5] But is it consistent to divorce the right of the magistrate or law-enforcement officer to bear arms—which sometimes must be used to kill—and

5. Dwight Ericsson, "New Testament Christianity and the Morality of Capital Punishment," *Journal of the American Scientific Affiliation* 14:79.

the right of a duly authorized court to pass the death penalty? Is there any difference in principle between the two? Beside this, from whence comes the authority for the officer to bear arms, if it indeed exists? If there is some scriptural basis for it, it cannot be Romans 13:4, for the right existed before Paul wrote. It must go back to Genesis 9:6 if it is to be traced to the Bible, and that text is manifestly a mandate for punishing murderers with death.

Perhaps Voltaire was more consistent than many abolitionists of later vintage. He recognized the mandate but admitted his reluctance to enforce it: "The sword of justice is committed to our hands; but, we ought rather to blunt than render its edge more keen. It remains in its sheath in the presence of royalty—'tis to admonish us that it should be rarely drawn."[6]

But, getting back to the sword of Romans 13:4, is such a sword merely a symbol of authority without any reference to execution? Are swords not used for execution? Evidence that this "sword" (Gk, *machaira*) must refer primarily to capital punishment is seen in the fact that it refers not to the dagger worn by Roman emperors—a sign of office—but to the sword worn by the superior magistrates of the provinces, to whom belonged the right of capital punishment.[7] The sword is not so much a symbol of capital punishment as it is the *instrument* of capital punishment. As such, therefore, it symbolizes the right of government to use force.

In conclusion, it should be pointed out that Paul appears to rest his concept of the authority of the state

6. Voltaire, "A Commentary on Crimes and Punishments," in *An Essay on Crimes and Punishments,* trans. E. D. Ingraham, (Stanford: Academic Reprints, 1952), p. 130.
7. Thus Marvin R. Vincent, *Word Studies in the New Testament* (Grand Rapids: Eerdmans, 1965), 3:164; and James Henry Thayer, *A Greek-English Lexicon of the New Testament* (1901 reprint, Grand Rapids: Baker, 1977), p. 393.

squarely on Genesis 9:6. The right of capital punishment, Paul seems to say, is at the very heart of government's power, and he clearly teaches that this is a derived authority in his concept of the magistrate as the "minister of God." The mandate given to Noah was very alive indeed!

1 Peter 2:13-14

The apostle Peter echoes the words of Paul regarding the Christian's attitude toward the state: "Submit yourselves for the Lord's sake to every human institution, whether to a king, as the one in authority, or to governors as sent by him for the punishment of evil-doers and the praise of those who do right" (1 Pet. 2:13-14). Though Peter makes no specific reference to the sword, his words "for the punishment of evil-doers" probably can be understood exactly the way Paul meant them in Romans 13:4. Peter uses the word *ekdikesin* (punishment), from the same root as Paul's word *ekdikos* (avenger) in Romans 13:4. It is reasonable to assume that Peter attached the same significance to the word, that is, "retribution" and ultimately capital punishment, especially since Peter was familiar with the writings of Paul and regarded them as Scripture (2 Pet. 3:15-16).

Revelation 13:10

The final possible reference to capital punishment is made by the apostle John in the book of Revelation: "If anyone is destined for captivity, to captivity he goes; if anyone kills with the sword, with the sword he must be killed. Here is the perseverance and the faith of the saints" (Rev. 13:10).

A textual problem exists in this passage that has a bearing upon the question of its being a valid reference to capital punishment. The King James Version, which used the Received Text as the basis of its translation, renders the verse, "He that leadeth into captivity, shall go into captivity: he that killeth with the sword must be killed with the sword." Translated in this way, the verse is a clear comfort to the saints persecuted by the beast described in the previous verses and identified by many as the Antichrist of the future. This comfort comes in terms of the certain retributive justice of God, which shall surely catch up with the persecutors of the saints.

However, faced with variations in important manuscripts, some scholars, like Alford, have adopted an alternate reading: "If anyone is for captivity, into captivity he goeth: if any to be slain with the sword, then he should be slain with the sword."[8] Beside certain manuscript evidence, this reading seems to be supported by Jeremiah 43:11, from which it may be quoted. The verse as such would constitute a statement of what God's people could expect rather than a statement of divine retribution.

The issue, of course, rests on which reading, "if any man is *to be killed*" or "if any man *shall kill*," is to be accepted, so that, in the latter case, a reference exists to retributive punishment by virtue of one's killing by the sword and having to be killed by the sword. In my judgment the manuscript evidence points to the reading "if any man shall kill," so that the thought of retributive justice is present.[9] John would be, in effect, quoting the words of Christ in Matthew 26:52 regarding the sword. Such a principle as retributive justice is best summed up in terms of capital punishment, though the distinction is here that the retribution is more divine than through human agency.

Revelation 13:10 is important principally for cumulative evidence, not as a crucial text. First Peter 2:13-14 is of similar importance. As a specific reference to capital punishment, Romans 13 is much clearer.

8. Henry Alford, *The Greek Testament,* (Boston: Lee & Shepherd, 1886), 4:678.
9 So also the RSV and NEB.

Conclusion

Chapters 6 and 7 have presented evidence to support the contention that capital punishment was recognized by Christ and His apostles as an enduring principle and a live mandate. A few closing words are now in order to sum up the significance of this portion of the book.

The mandate of capital punishment means that God has delegated authority to human government so that, if necessary in the course of its proper function, it may use force and may exercise the death penalty. This authority must be used in the interests of justice as set forth in the Word of God and not for purposes of oppression.

It is imperative to recognize the source of the state's authority. God is the source of all rights, and He sovereignly dispenses them—in the case of capital punishment, to the civil magistrate. As such the magistrate carries out the divine will. The state, although serving in such a capacity, is not by virtue of the right justified in the misuse of this power. The transmission of authority does not necessarily carry with it moral character as well. The state does not possess the divine attribute of holiness.

Therefore, the question of how far the Christian can go in obedience to the state is also present. The limitation of the power is in what is contrary to the will of God. We are to "render to Caesar" the things that are his. But "Caesar" can go beyond his proper jurisdiction. When such a time comes, obedience is no longer required.

The point is that capital punishment is within these limits. A challenge to such justice is a form of civil disobedience, not civil reform.

Another possibility that has been discussed in this section is that capital punishment is not only a divinely delegated mandate, but it may be foundational to human government, especially when extended to the crime of insurrection. It is noteworthy that in some countries, for example, Russia and Great Britain, where capital punishment has been abolished, it still exists as a punishment for certain crimes against the state. Though not clear from Genesis 9:6, we have seen implied in such passages as John 19 and Romans 13 that the state indeed has the right to punish crimes against itself with the death penalty.

Part 3

The Purpose
of Capital Punishment

8
The Primary Purpose: Justice

At the heart of the controversy over capital punishment is the philosophical debate over its purpose or function. Some would limit its function only to the greatest human good. Such is the position of those who hold a utilitarian philosophy of the law. Cesare Beccaria reflects this philosophy, which also traces the source of law to the will of society rather than divine commandments: "Laws . . . are only the sum of the smallest portions of the private liberty of each individual, and represent the general will, which is the aggregate of that of each individual."[1] He then goes on to ask, "Did anyone ever give others the right of taking away his life?"[2]

"Utilitarianism" is the ethical theory that holds that the rightness of an action is determined by whether or not it

1. Cesare Beccaria, "On Crime and Punishment," in *An Essay on Crimes and Punishments,* trans. E. D. Ingraham (Stanford: Academic Reprints, 1952), p. 97.
2. Ibid.

achieves the greatest good for the greatest number of people. The term originated with Jeremy Bentham and was given its classic expression by John Stuart Mill, who deduced from the principle of utilitarianism that since all punishment involves pain and is therefore evil, it ought only to be admitted so far as it promises to exclude some greater evil.[3] John Austin, the great English jurist, furthered the cause of utilitarianism in his work *The Province of Jurisprudence Determined* (1832), in which he distinguished between law and morality. That distinction was welcomed by such Americans as J. C. Gray and Oliver Wendell Holmes as a major clarification between law and morality.

With such works as these, humanitarian thinkers were able to drive a wedge between criminal justice and the "natural moral law." According to E. L. H. Taylor, this had the following profound effect:

> The thin end of this wedge to detach the idea of justice entirely from its theological context and religious roots was the theory that because all human laws vary so much from place to place and from time to time, they must all be considered purely relative and therefore changeable. . . . Justice from that moment ceased to be revered as an end in itself.[4]

I contend in this book, however, that justice and law are rooted in a divine standard. Whenever we say, "That is just," or, "That is unjust," we have, consciously or unconsciously, admitted the existence of a fixed standard, because frequently this affirmation has no connection with our own private advantage or the so-called advantage of society but simply witnesses to a "law of nature" within

---

3. John Stuart Mill, *Utilitarianism,* Great Books of the Western World (Chicago: Encyclopedia Britannica, 1955), 43:472-76.
4. E. L. H. Taylor, "The Death Penalty," *Essays on the Death Penalty,* ed. T. Robert Ingram (Houston: St. Thomas Press, 1963), p. 34.

us.[5] Such an absolute is being denied today.

In most discussions of capital punishment, the question of justice seldom comes up. Usually, the issue is resolved on utilitarian grounds such as reformation, deterrence, or sentimental appeals to the value of human life and miscarriages of justice. The following discussion will approach the issue of the purpose of capital punishment by dealing first with justice as its primary purpose. Consequently, other purposes, such as the establishment of the sanctity of human life and the deterrence of crime, will be treated as derivative and, thus, of secondary value. Finally, the problem of human fallability or the miscarriage of justice will be dealt with because of its bearing upon the question of the implementation of the death penalty.

THE ESTABLISHMENT OF JUSTICE

The primary function of the death penalty is to establish or to satisfy justice (Rom. 13:4—the basic meaning of "avenge"). Capital punishment represents retributive justice pure and simple, because it cannot have any corrective benefits to the one put to death, at least as far as this life is concerned. Theologians call this kind of punishment "retribution." It will be the purpose of these pages to demonstrate that there is a place for retributive justice, but in order to accomplish this, it will be necessary first to distinguish between retribution and revenge. Next, it will be shown that human government has as its ultimate purpose the dispensing of justice. The Mosaic *lex talionis,* law of retribution, also comes to bear upon the issue. Each of these, therefore, will be considered in that order before any attempt is made to justify the concept of retribution.

---

5 C S Lewis's discussion of this fact is helpful. *Mere Christianity* (New York: Macmillan, 1960), pp. 17-35.

THE QUESTION OF REVENGE

Justice has been defined as a just rendering to every man his due. Similar to this idea of justice is the concept of retribution, which means the dispensing of reward or punishment according to the deserts of the individual. Retribution, however, is often confused with a kind of personal retaliation. Such is the case, for example, in the following quotation:

> The idea of punishment solely as retribution, which is merely a polite word for revenge, is gradually disappearing. This idea is yielding to the more modern, progressive and scientific attitude that retribution is not justification for any system of punishment, nor are its results beneficial.[6]

Such a statement seems to ignore the basic idea of justice as rendering to a man what he deserves and reflects the modern thinking on the question of responsibility, which will be discussed later in this chapter. Apparently, the word *retribution* represents an evil desire for revenge to another writer also: "But even if we agree that murder is the most wicked of crimes, that seems relevant only for a retributive theory of justice, not one based on deterrence. Today we don't like to say that we inflict punishment merely for vengeance."[7] But is retribution to be so glibly identified with vengeance in this sense and thus dismissed?

The theological meaning of retribution. Theologically, the term *retribution* usually refers to *eternal* retribution. This can be thought of in terms of God's response to

6. Evelle J. Younger, "A Sharp Medicine Reconsidered," in *Capital Punishment,* ed. Grant S. McClellan (New York: H. W. Wilson, 1961), p. 18.
7. H. P. Weihofen, "Urge to Punish," *Pastoral Psychology* 9 (June 1958): 32.

those who refuse to repent and therefore receive the just due of their sins, or it may refer to the Calvinistic doctrine that holds that some are rejected whom God does not elect to salvation. There is no reputable Calvinist theologian who suspects the least trace of spiteful vengeance in this act, and no theologian—either Calvinist or Arminian—who believes in eternal retribution considers such punishment to be anything other than just, because it is administered by a just God.

Scriptural teaching of retribution. A number of New Testament terms contribute to the scriptural concept of retribution. The Greek words *ekdikeo, ekdikesis,* and *ekdikos,* translated "to avenge," "vengeance," and "avenger" respectively, contain no thought of spiteful retaliation. For example, *ekdikos* is used in Romans 13:4 as a description of the civil magistrate who carries out the just retribution of the law. Other words, *orge* and *thumos,* refer to wrath attributed to God, whereas *kolasis* and *timoria* are translated "punishment," and *krino* and its derivatives are translated "judgment." All these words speak of the natural consequences of sin, not vengeful retaliation of an evil sort.

In the Old Testament, the most usual word for avenging is *naqam,* which first appears in Genesis 4:15 in reference to vengeance being taken on Cain. Personal and private revenge was forbidden to Israel in Leviticus 19:18. In the Old Testament the Lord's vengeance is regarded as retribution but not as retaliation. "It is set forth not as an *evil passion,* but rather as the righteous and unerring vindication of His own people and of His own course of action, to the discomfiture of those who had set themselves in opposition to Him."[8]

Retribution is properly a satisfaction or, according to the ancient figure of justice and her scales, a restoration

8. Robert B. Girdlestone, *Synonyms of the Old Testament* (Grand Rapids: Eerdmans, 1948), p. 255.

of a disturbed equilibrium. As such it is a proper, legitimate, and moral concept. Scripture makes a clear line of distinction between this doctrine and feelings of personal hatred by forbidding such feelings and the actions to which they would lead. Capital punishment as a form of retribution is a dictate of the moral nature, which demands that there should be a just portion between the offense and the penalty.

There is an instinctive justice seen in people who take the law into their own hands when an atrocious murder has been committed.

The popular meaning of revenge. Superficially viewed, revenge is the impulse to return blow for blow. When a person is injured, anger prompts him to inflict the same injury upon the one who injured him. But many circumstances can enter into the picture so that this basic simplicity is complicated, and a heavier blow or more severe injury is inflicted than was received. Revenge can thus defeat its own end—that an equal injury should be returned for an injury. There is the germ of a moral feeling in this in the sense of resentment, and there is a demand for a free, unrestrained existence, which is the condition of moral life.

Revenge and Genesis 9:6. Sometimes it is claimed that the language of Genesis 9:6 gives rise to personal revenge. The custom of the avenger of blood and the inevitable occasions in which personal vengefulness would enter into his duty has seemed to substantiate this claim. It is doubtful that Genesis 9:6 really teaches or allows for such vengeance. It is true that the punishment of the murderer is the responsibility of "man" universally. However, because all the judicial relations and ordinances of the increasing race were rooted in those of the family, and thus grew by a natural process out of that, the family relations furnished the basis for the closer definition of the word *man*. Therefore, the command does not sanction revenge but lays the foundation for the judicial rights of government (Rom. 13:1). This is substantiated by the phrase *image of God,* which limits the infliction of punishment so that it was not left to the whim of individuals but belonged to those who sought for justice and who therefore represent the authority and majesty of God.

The attempts to discredit retributive punishment by connecting or identifying it with the motive of revenge are fallacious. We can only admit a connection on the basis of the impulse to restore a disturbed order—a loss of balance in the equilibrium of justice. This impulse may admittedly be obscured by passion, but it has an objective basis in justice. Punishment puts things back into their right order. In this way retributive punishment becomes more objective in character.

THE RELATION OF JUSTICE TO HUMAN GOVERNMENT

The fact that human government has been delegated the divine power of life over death has been demonstrated from Scripture. This power is the basis for all the other legitimate rights of government in the opinion of many. This chapter purposes to determine the relationship of the Christian ethic to civil government and to show how justice is the aim of the divinely ordained "powers that be," a purpose that contrasts to that of the church. If justice is the divinely ordained purpose of human government, and capital punishment is a divine mandate, then the function of government is weakened by the abolition of capital punishment.

THE RELATION OF THE CHRISTIAN ETHIC TO GOVERNMENT

Two extremes are prevalent in Christian thinking about the state. Both represent a denial of the legitimate, separate functions of church and state. One extreme is that government is totally evil and that the Christian has no place in it whatsoever. The other viewpoint, and the more prevalent, is that it is the task of Christianity so to influence society and government as to bring the Christian's personal ethic into the application of its laws and attitudes. Those who advocate this viewpoint may speak in terms of the "leaven" of Christianity having such an effect upon society as to make the practice of capital punishment "obsolete." Part and parcel of this latter view is an insistence that rehabilitation must be the primary purpose of penal institutions. But the question is, Can there be any lasting rehabilitation without also satisfying justice?

There is a contrast between the state and the church that is entirely intentional and right. It is similar to the contrast between law and grace. Though law presupposes grace in the sense that grace cannot be demonstrated apart from the satisfying of the law, the two are not intended to be mixed or confused. But can the Christian ethic, which condemns personal vengeance, apply to the state, which, strictly speaking, is not Christian?

If the Christian ethic is not intended, therefore, to Christianize the state in the sense of the state's employing only the principles of love and grace in its function, is there any relationship at all between the Christian ethic and the state? There is, but only in the sense that there is a relation between *justice* and the Christian ethic. In other words, God is able to act in grace to the Christian—and thereby able to command His people to do likewise in all their personal dealings—because the requirements of justice have been met in Christ. God can forgive because the penalty for man's crimes against His law have been paid by the death of Christ as the believer's substitute. God's grace, therefore, presupposes the fulfilling of justice. The Christian message concerns the grace of God but not to the neglect of the justice of God. The Christian ethic should have its influence on human government, therefore, in terms of influencing govern-

ment to dispense justice properly, while not losing sight
of mercy when the case warrants it. The Christian ethic
must have its impact in terms of the righteousness of the
gospel rather than in terms of the grace of the gospel as
far as the state is concerned. Government can only act
righteously as far as its principal aim is concerned.

Both church and state cease to fulfill their divinely
ordained roles when they seek to enter into the sphere
of the other and dictate the other's function in terms of
its own.

Romans 12 and 13 serve as the finest scriptural efforts
to distinguish between the two respective spheres of
church and state. The state belongs to the natural order,
hence the words "every human soul" appear in Romans
13:1 in the exhortation to be subject to the powers that
be. The church is spiritual and presupposes faith (Rom.
12:1-6). The one has justice as its principle obligation;
the other, love. To the state belongs the means of con-
straint, in order to demand of every man the duties of
justice. To the church belongs the reign of liberty or
spontaneous love, which cannot be required of anyone.
There is a profound distinction between the state and the
church, according to Paul's teaching, but there is not an
opposition. The law paves the way for grace, and the
conscientious practice of justice prepares one for the
demonstration of love. The state represses crime and
preserves public order, so that the church can pursue its
work without interference. That work is the transforma-
tion of the citizens of this earth into citizens of heaven.
There is thus a reciprocal relationship between the two
institutions.

The viewpoint of some Christians, which does not recognize clearly defined and complementary spheres of
human government and the church, has led to some

forms of pacifism and, of course, the movement to abolish capital punishment. Since each of these, carnal conflict and retributive justice, seems to be in conflict with the Christian ethic that they wish to see the state adopt, they withdraw themselves from much participation in the state, though they submit to its laws. The question we pose, however, is this: If the state has a legitimate role separate from but not opposed to the church, can Christians not participate so long as they do not violate their consciences?

Actually, the Scriptures seem to teach that the state's function is a noble one, and this is due to its original mandate. For this reason, Paul speaks of the magistrate as a "minister" of God. The Pauline concept is much loftier than the concept of those who rest the right of the state on utilitarian grounds. To Paul, the state has divine principles as its foundation, and it is intended to be essentially a moral institution. Conscience is assigned as the ground for obedience to the state (Rom. 13:5), and this ground is the very limit of this obedience. For when the state, which is supposed to govern under the ordinance of God, orders something contrary to the will of God, then protest is in order. But this protest must continue to render respect to the principle of the state in the manner in which the protest is lodged and, when necessary, be characterized by calmness when punishment is borne.

The Rome of Paul's day eventually became anti-Christian. But this persecution was more personal than official. Persecution did not represent the judicial policy as it did the animosity of individuals. Justice in this case was thwarted, and Rome misused its power, ceasing in this instance to fulfill its role. It must not be forgotten that in the beginning Christians like Paul enjoyed an official benevolence and thrived under official protection.

Human government has been ordained of God for the purpose of dispensing justice, because of the depravity of man. Due to this depravity, force must often be exercised. This is the power of the sword of Romans 13:4. Such force may contrast with the message of the gospel, but it is necessary. No state is able long to dispense with the sword.

The failure of the state always to administer justice consistently is no cause for the abolition of capital punishment. For example, some say that they favor abolition on grounds that the lack of justice in the present American jury system makes proper administration of the death penalty impossible. In the light of the purpose of government, there is more at stake than the possible miscarriage of justice. If the system is not working properly, it needs to be reformed. But to do away with a necessary law on the basis of the failure to enforce it properly perpetrates more than a miscarriage of justice—it does away with justice altogether. The loss of the concept of justice in modern thinking is partly the cause of increases in crime. In the light of biblical teaching on the sinful nature of men and the current increase in crime, it is frightening that people should be thinking of measures that relax the laws and even do away with some, such as capital punishment. The nation is reaping the harvest of permissiveness and the loss of biblical justice. "Righteousness exalts a nation, but sin is a disgrace to any people" (Prov. 14:34).

9
Implications of Retribution

THE LEX TALIONIS

The Hebrew *lex talionis,* law of retaliation, is a literal application of the concept of retribution. It is stated in Exodus 21:23-25 as follows: "But if there is any further injury, then you shall appoint as a penalty life for life, eye for eye, tooth for tooth, hand for hand, foot for foot, burn for burn, wound for wound, bruise for bruise." This law applied only to freemen, for the next verse, Exodus 21:26, says that a slave may go free rather than demand the exact retaliation of his master.

The *lex talionis* is generally regarded as a considerable advance over earlier practice and was enunciated not only to sanction stern penalties but also to protect offenders from excessive punishments. The *lex talionis,* though simple and severe, has profound meaning. It represents the concept in justice in which a judicial sentence is essentially a process of restoration of the just order, which has become unstable.

Obviously, though, there will be cases in which this direct restoration will not be humanly possible. For example, the lost eye cannot be restored to its socket. At this point, many believe that the *lex talionis* as stated is to be taken symbolically and not literally—that like destruction is not intended, but rather like restoration. Is it a general precept that is intended to regulate the principle? This may be substantiated by the fact that these precise forms (eye for eye) were not, in actual practice, a part of Jewish law. Like for like is the principle; but when in the case of lower offenses there might be equivalents, convenience and other circumstances might determine their reception without violating the spirit of the maxim. Against such a "spiritualization" of the *lex talionis*, however, is the clear language of Scripture and the fact that a literal interpretation, though admittedly severe, would be reasonable in terms of its meaning. Added to this is the statement of Exodus 21:26, where an alternative to the severity of the *lex talionis* is offered to the master of an injured slave, that is, the slave's being set free. Actually, though, the practice of capital punishment rests on firmer ground than the *lex talionis* alone.

The *lex talionis* represents a universal divine principle. In the New Testament, the same idea of sure retribution is expressed by Galatians 6:7: "whatever a man sows, this he will also reap." As such, the *lex talionis* presented, at that stage of revelation, the mind of God regarding an eternal principle, that of retribution. Can murder be excluded from such a universal rule?

Jesus' repeal of the *lex talionis* was a repeal in terms of personal retaliation on the part of the candidate for the kingdom of heaven, and the teaching of Paul in Romans 12:19 confirms this ethic for the Christian. However, it was shown from Romans 13:4 that the law of retribution or retaliation was valid for constituted civil authority as a necessary element for its function. In terms of justice and civil government, therefore, the *lex talionis* is still in effect and is expressed by the continuing mandate of capital punishment.

THE PLACE OF RETRIBUTIVE PUNISHMENT

Modern theories of justice are the product of the theory of relativity applied to morals. In such relativistic systems, society becomes the standard of justice. Often the appeal is made to the fact that concepts of justice vary much from nation to nation and from time to time, and that even on the question or murder there is much difference of opinion as to what constitutes just punishment.

This book does not pretend to offer solutions to the problems surrounding the implementation of the death penalty, such as degrees of homicide or the definition of legal insanity. But my conviction is strong that the modern theorists are beginning at the wrong point; their refusal to accept a fixed, absolute standard undergirding all justice has led them to the place of permissiveness and nihilism. The starting point and continuing standard of justice is the Word of God, not the subjective conclusions of utilitarians. Biblical justice is retributive justice.

Sometimes humanitarian concerns in law are in basic opposition to the essence of civil law that is intended to issue restraints and punish violators. Justice should be the first concern of law, and all other concerns should be subordinate. In other words, the primary function of the act of punishment is retribution. Some humanitarians would give the impression, of course, that most people are being punished for their misfortunes rather than for their guilt and thus attempt to discredit the retributive purpose of punishment in this manner. But only those who are free moral agents experience punishment, and the question is, What is "punishment"?

Some would answer this question with the word *rehabilitation*. They maintain, in an apparent disregard for history, that so-called Christian influences have been responsible for this attitude. For example, in a report entitled "Punishment," prepared by the Church of England, there seems to be a reluctance to trace the idea of retributive punishment to anything but medieval barbarism. Nevertheless, the report seems forced to conclude:

> Retributive punishment may arise from moral insights. Certain behaviour. . . obliges us, the retributionists would say, as a matter of moral obligation to perform another sort of behaviour (the "punishment"). On this view retribution would be the *raison d'etre* of punishment, deterrence and reformation being byproducts. As and when retribution has this moral basis there can clearly be a balancing of the retributive, reforming and deterrent features of a particular situation. But all this presupposes that the law expresses moral insights.[1]

But this is the crux of the matter; the law *should* express moral insights gained from the Word of God.

RETRIBUTION AND ETERNAL PUNISHMENT

No discussion of the place of retributive punishment can honestly avoid the connections in principle between capital punishment as pure retribution on the human plane and eternal retribution on the spiritual plane. If there is a legitimate place for eternal retribution in evangelical theology—and no evangelical can deny this and remain truly evangelical—then there is certainly a place for retributive punishment on the human plane, that is, a form of punishment in which there is no reformatory purpose whatsoever. Or, to put it another way, if an evangelical Christian can see the validity and place of eternal punishment and deny that there is any place on the tem-

---

1. Church of England, National Assembly, Board for Social Responsibility, *Punishment* (The Church Information Office, 1963), p. 13.

poral level for any punishment that does not have reformation as its goal, he is inconsistent. To admit one is to
open the door for the possibility, indeed the need, for
the other, because it keeps the distinction between punishment and rehabilitation absolutely clear.

When speaking of eternal retribution, William G. T.
Shedd, the great Reformed theologian of the last genera-
tion, could not resist a few remarks on capital punishment:

> The human penalty that approaches nearest to the Divine,
> is capital punishment. There is more of the purely retribu-
> tive element in this than in any other. The reformatory
> element is wanting. And this punishment has a kind of
> endlessness. Death is a finality. It forever separates the
> murderer from earthly society, even as further punishment
> separates forever from the society of God and heaven.[2]

He noted a further similarity between the two in reference to the question of reformation:

> Early was the question raised, whether the suffering to
> which Christ sentences the wicked is for the purpose of
> correcting and educating the transgressor, or of vindicat-
> ing and satisfying the law he has broken: a question which
> is the key to the whole controversy. For if the individual
> criminal is of greater concern than the universal law, then
> the suffering must refer principally to him and his inter-
> ests. But if the law is of more importance than any individ-
> ual, then the suffering must refer principally to it.[3]

It is beyond the scope of this book to attempt an ex-
haustive defense of eternal punishment. However, to
some extent, the justification of eternal punishment has a

2. William G. T. Shedd, *Dogmatic Theology* (Grand Rapids: Zondervan, n.d.), 2:716.
3. Ibid., 2:668-69.

bearing on the justification of pure retribution, so that some points should be made at this time.

Jesus Christ Himself was the Person most responsible for the doctrine of eternal perdition. Careful exegesis of all the relevant passages will produce a concept that depicts such punishment as conscious and eternal and from which there is no recovery. Two representative passages are Matthew 25:41, 46, which speaks of eternal punishment, and Luke 16:28, which speaks of a place of torment.

In answer to the question Is not retributive punishment an idea wrong in itself? C. S. Lewis says that the answer is negative, because all punishment is basically retributive, not reformatory or deterrent. No one has the right strictly to punish merely for reformatory and deterrent purposes. Unless a man deserves to be punished, he ought not be made to suffer. Nothing can be more immoral than to inflict suffering on a man who does not deserve it, for the purpose either of improving him or deterring others. Furthermore, what else can God do with a man who has always lived a hellish life? God cannot condone this evil. To condone it would amount to treating evil as if it were good.[4]

RETRIBUTION AND HUMAN DIGNITY AND RESPONSIBILITY

Retributive punishment actually puts human dignity on a high level. The theory that teaches that punishment merely is expedient and useful degrades human nature. When justice is at the basis of penalty, man is treated in dignity, as a person. However, if the public good is the basis, he is treated as a means to an end. Man has free choice and responsibility, and punishment based on this assumption honors man for what he really is.

4. C. S. Lewis, *The Problem of Pain* (New York: Macmillan, 1944), pp. 108-9.

Responsibility is at the basis of all punishment, and any failure to recognize that degrades human personality. As it stands, the law recognizes basic human dignity and the worth of the individual. In countries where this concept is denied, the individual usually has no rights. It is possible that the scientific humanist concept of man, which underlies modern sociology and penology, will lead eventually to just such a denial of human rights. Only the concept of man as the image of God can guarantee these rights.

No punishment can really be justified apart from retributive grounds. If the idea of just desert and retribution are excluded and only deterrence or rehabilitation remains as a valid ground for punishment, there is no reason whatsoever that the pain of punishment should be confined to the actual doer of the wrong deed. It would be just as logical to extend it to his children and wife.

There is in this same connection a growing trend to look at responsibility more in terms of the social environment. A criminal, some say, should not be punished for being raised in a slum or in a home which might have been abnormal as to have breeded the causes of the crime which he commits. Environment certainly plays a part in crime, but such a doctrine overlooks the biblical teaching that regardless of his circumstances man is responsible to some degree for his choices.

For example, Romans 1:20 implies that certain truths concerning God are evident to all men, regardless of their personal situation. This evidence of God is a sufficient basis for God to judge all men righteously. In Romans 2:14 all men are said to have an inward witness to right and wrong. This suggests the idea that men will be judged according to the light they have.

It is at this point that the relation between responsibility and environment comes into proper focus. Each man will be judged individually by God on the basis of his "works" (Rev. 20:12). Thus each man's situation will be taken into account, but his ultimate responsibility will never be precluded by his environment, only qualified. The judgment referred to here, of course, has no relation to the question of eternal salvation, which is decided purely on the basis of personal faith, not works.

Since no mercy is allowed by the Bible for premeditated, malicious murder, however, it seems inescapable that we must conclude that for that particular crime, a man is fully responsible. On the other hand, Scripture recognizes such a thing as accidental homicide. Thus a degree of responsibility is seen in that particular case.

Basically, there are four biblical assumptions in our legal system regarding responsibility: (1) everyone, except children and the legally insane, knows the difference between right and wrong; (2) everyone, apart from children and the legally insane, is able to choose between doing right and wrong (in spite of original sin, man retains a relative measure of moral freedom); (3) anyone who chooses to do wrong should be properly punished for it, and the state must punish men only for the *crimes* they commit; and (4) no one should be punished unless in actual fact he has committed some definite crime (retributive punishment).[5]

What about the insanity plea? Is such a thing consistent with good psychiatry or biblical teaching about man's responsibility?

So far as psychiatry is concerned, there is no complete agreement among psychiatrists on the meaning of mental illness. According to C. R. Jeffery in his book *Criminal Responsibility and Mental Disease*,[6] some use "mental illness" as a synonym for "psychosis," whereas others include neurotic disorders and personality disorders.

---

5. E. L. H. Taylor, "Medicine or Morals as the Basis of Justice and Law," in *Essays on the Death Penalty*, ed. Ingram (Houston: St. Thomas Press, 1963), pp. 90-93.
6. C. R. Jeffery, *Criminal Responsibility and Mental Disease* (Springfield, Ill.: Charles C. Thomas, 1967), pp. 36-48.

Mental illness thus gets expanded to include sociopaths, alcoholics, and drug addicts.

Another fact complicates the question. The legal definition of insanity depends on the jurisdiction within which the defendant is being tried. Two standards are used: the "M'Naghten" rule (1843) and the "Durham" rule (1954). The M'Naghten rule states: "The jurors ought to be told in all cases that every man is presumed to be sane and to possess a sufficient degree of reason to be responsible for his crimes, until the contrary is proven."

The Durham rule merely asks whether the defendant had a mental illness or defect at the time of the crime. This same rule is involved in those questions of whether a defendant is capable of standing trial at a given time due to mental illness.

Finally, there is the further complicating phenomenon of the question in the minds of some minority psychiatrists like Thomas S. Szasz of whether or not there is such a thing as mental illness at all.[7] Corresponding to this opinion is the Christian psychologist Jay Adams,[8] who calls attention to the fact that Scripture has nothing to say about the modern psychiatric categories such as schizophrenia and paranoia. On the other hand, Szasz, coming from a strictly nonreligious point of view, holds that the so-called mentally ill are always shamming or counterfeiting through their bizarre behavior. Both men agree that these people can become "victimized" and locked into their condition, even though it is self-induced.

Such "mentally ill" people, then, may not be able to control themselves after a certain point. Are they then no longer responsible? The Scriptures assume that those whom it says should be punished for sin or crime are

7. Thomas S. Szasz, *The Myth of Mental Illness* (New York: Hoeber-Harper, 1961).
8. Jay E. Adams, *Competent to Counsel* (Grand Rapids: Eerdmans, 1970), pp. 26-36.

responsible creatures, and it makes no explicit provision for any exceptions.

The Bible does make passing references to "madness," but most of those references are to irrational behavior rather than a settled condition of mental illness described by the modern medical profession. Paul was once accused of madness due to his great learning (Acts 26:24), and Paul warned the Corinthians that visitors to some of their wilder charismatic sessions might suppose that they were mad (1 Cor. 14:23). In none of these cases is anyone implied to have been without responsibility for what he was doing, at least ultimately.

What is the sum of it? Since Western civilization has allowed historically for a certain possibility that some people committed acts for which they could not be held responsible, and most Christian psychologists acknowledge the same, it would probably be rash to rule out such a thing altogether.

The Bible seems to allow for very little bad behavior on the part of people who could not be considered responsible, and thus the modern legal system has undoubtedly gone far astray in failing to punish some murderers. Most modern views of man rest on assumptions that are radically unbiblical, which gradually give up the dignity that belongs to rational creatures by saying that all crime is perpetrated by "sick people." The policy, then, should be a healthy scepticism toward every plea of "not guilty by reason of insanity."

RETRIBUTION AND REHABILITATION

Rehabilitation or reform is the attempt on the part of penal institutions to salvage the life of the criminal and fit him for the resumption of citizenship. Penologists have believed for many years that some responsibility lies upon penal institutions to attempt to rehabilitate the criminal.

But the pendulum of thinking that once regarded prisons and jails as places of deprivation and torture is in danger of swinging to the other extreme—that rehabilitation must not only be the right but the mandatory experience of every convict. This rehabilitation will be best accomplished by a corps of trained psychiatrists who will be qualified to deal with the mental aberrations of the criminal mind. When this rehabilitation is complete in the judgment of these doctors, the convict can safely return to society.

It is important to note a difference between the reformatory benefits of a punishment given primarily for retributive purposes and "punishment" inflicted solely for corrective or developmental ends. Though personal improvement may result from the infliction of a penalty, this consequence should not be confused with the purpose that is purely retributive. When a punishment is administered soley for the purpose of rehabilitation with no clear reference to guilt and retribution, the criminal is being deprived of the process in which he approves of the just retribution of the law and repents of his crime. This would be the extreme of the type of penal thinking growing in prominence today. It is doubtful whether rehabilitation could take place within a system that ignores the necessity of repentance based on recognition of deserved punishment.

Another argument against capital punishment is that of the possibility of a murderer's repentance and salvation had he been permitted to live. For example, Menno Simons, who certainly held a biblical view of salvation, nevertheless argued against the death penalty on the grounds of possible eventual conversion of the convict. He wrote:

> If he remain impenitent and his life be taken, one would unmercifully rob him of the time of repentance of which, in case his life were spared, he might yet avail himself. It

would be unmerciful to tyranically offer his poor soul which was purchased with such precious treasure to the devil of hell, under unbearable judgment, punishment, and the wrath of God, so that he would forever have to suffer and bear the tortures of the unquenchable burning, the consuming fire, eternal pain, woe, and death.[9]

If, however, one holds a view of the sovereignty of God in which all the elect will be saved (e.g., Rom. 8:30), he need not be concerned about this objection.

The Christian should be concerned about the salvation of the murderer, but perhaps from another perspective entirely. Allowing the murderer to live, thus failing to meet the requirements of justice, could do a great *injustice* to him in this life. Physical life, after all, is not man's most valuable possession. A man's opportunity to repent and prepare for eternity is his most valuable possession. Laxity in regard to the death penalty is not necessarily conducive to the repentance of the criminal. He may or may not become converted, regardless of the penalty of death, but the certainty of the death penalty provides what one writer calls a "secondary measure of the love of God."[10]

The concept that penal institutions have the sole purpose of education is not in keeping with two facts: (1) people of high intellect and more education are capable of terrible crimes, and (2) the grace of God in salvation, or at least the moral repentance of the criminal, are the answers to evil.

The church has the best ingredient for lasting rehabilitation: spiritual regeneration. Many, of course, can be rehabilitated to some extent apart from a spiritual approach. However, the church misses a great opportunity

9. Meno Simons, "Reply to Martin Micron," in *The Complete Writings of Menno Simons* (Scottdale: Herald Press, 1956), p. 921.
10. Carey, "A Bible Study," in *Essays on the Death Penalty*, ed. Ingram (Houston: St. Thomas Press, 1963), p. 116.

if it fails to make its contribution toward rehabilitation and leaves it to the state.

Lewis writes of what he considers a possible danger in the modern concept of rehabilitation. This humanitarian theory of punishment, he says, is proposed by its advocates as a mild and merciful approach to crime. Despite its claim to serve humanity, in reality it is a dangerous illusion and disguises the possibility of cruelty and injustice in the extreme. Lewis urges a return to the retributional theory in the interests of the criminal. His argument can be summarized as follows:

The humanitarian theory of punishment deprives the lawbreaker of the rights of a human being in several ways. First, it removes from the punishment the concept of desert. Desert is the only connecting link between punishment and justice. Only as it is deserved or undeserved can a punishment be just or unjust.

Second, the humanitarian theory can be concerned only with two questions: Will it deter crime? and, Will it reform?

Third, the length and nature of sentences will be determined by those considered to be qualified; that is, scientists trained in that branch of medicine, not in jurisprudence. The problem of determining sentences will no longer be a moral problem, but a question of when such a qualified person considers the criminal to be "cured."

Fourth, no one else—jurist, Christian, or theologian—will be able to say, "This punishment is unjust, he does not deserve it." Sentences will be removed from the hands of jurists responsible to the public and will be placed into the hands of technical experts whose sciences do not take into account such categories as rights or justice. Adherents to this theory argue that since this transfer of responsibility implies the abandonment of the old idea of punishment, which entailed vindictive motives, it will be safe to leave criminals in such hands. But such an argument overlooks the biblical idea of man's fallen nature.

Fifth, the "cures" will be compulsory, imposed with or without the desire of the criminal.

Sixth, the "cure" could be faked. Indeed, under certain conceivable circumstances, great efforts to fool one's captors into believing a cure has been effected would be inevitable. Treatment could become an unbearable experience that could far exceed any ordinary punishment a criminal might deserve, but desert is a concept that the humanitarian theory has discarded.

Seventh, when justified on the basis of deterrence with no basis in desert, the morality of the punishment disappears. It is not even necessary that the man should have committed the crime. The deterrent effect demands that the public should draw the moral only. The state could conceivably fake a trial. Any distaste for such justice on the part of the humanitarian would be inconsistent with his own theory, for distaste would betray the kind of conscience arising out of the retributive theory of punishment.

Finally, the possibility of evil rulers armed with such a humanitarian theory of punishment and rehabilitation must be taken into account. If crime and disease are to be regarded as the same thing, it follows that any state of mind that leaders choose to call "disease" can be treated as crime and compulsorily "cured." Some schools of psychology already regard religion as a neurosis.[11]

For rehabilitation to be effected in any given case, there must be the recognition on the part of the individual that his punishment is just and deserved. This is involved in the biblical concept of repentance. The offender must see the law of retribution in his act of crime

11. C. S. Lewis, "The Humanitarian Theory of Punishment," in *Churchmen Speak* (Appleford Abingdon Berkshire: Marcham Manor, 1966), pp. 39-44.

and become convinced of his guilt before he will desire correction. Such a process would be lacking in the modern concept of rehabilitation.

There is biblical evidence that a man guilty of such a crime as murder is not to be considered as a candidate for rehabilitation, especially if he himself is oriented by the biblical concept of justice and retribution. Proverbs 28:17, for example, says, "A man who is laden with the guilt of human blood Will be a fugitive until death; let no one support him." The verse is cast, historically, into the times of the "avenger of blood," when the murderer was involved in a ceaseless flight to escape vengeance. The warning was to anyone who might seek to give him aid or comfort, for his only rest lay in the fulfillment of justice in death.

Retribution and Love

Some opponents to the death penalty believe that the demand for retributive justice is not compatible with the idea of Christian love—that retribution had its place in terms of informing man about the seriousness and consequences of his sins, but that love must now supersede the idea of retribution. Usually this idea recognizes the need for *some* punishment. They believe, however, that love cannot be shown to one condemned to die, so that the cross should replace justice with the quality of love or infuse the concern of love into retribution. In other words, the state must draw the line at capital punishment, for her retribution would prevent the showing of love.

What these people fail to realize is that retribution must *precede* any display of love—that love presupposes just retribution. Retribution is the primary concern of law and must be met. Love cannot be demonstrated until the law and justice have been first satisfied. God's purpose in justice is not superseded by His purpose in love. God always had one purpose—His glory—and this purpose was to be fulfilled in harmony with both justice and love.

The relationship of retributive justice to love is best indicated in the crucifixion itself. The death of Christ was necessary in terms of retribution for the sins of the world before God could demonstrate His grace in saving those who by faith accept Christ's death as the just retribution for their own sins. The death of Christ is therefore the basis for the manifestation of the love of God. Abolitionists reason away or ignore the necessity for retribution. In doing so, they unwittingly undermine the whole biblical concept of retributive justice. The work of Christ on the cross for the sins of the world rests on this concept. Consciously or unconsciously, the reasoning behind the abolition of capital punishment strikes at the very heart of the theology of the atonement.

Retribution and the Sanctity of Life

The sanctity of human life is incorporated into the very institution of capital punishment in Genesis 9:6 in such a way as to imply that it is one of the basic reasons for retribution. In other words, retributive justice is an indicator of the sacredness of life.

THE MEANING OF SANCTITY

It is believed by most commentators that the clause attached to the mandate for the punishment of the murderer by man in Genesis 9:6, "For in the image of God He made man," constitutes a reason for God's demanding the death penalty. The idea of the offense to God has already been considered, but it will now be appropriate to look at this in terms of the sanctity of life as it relates to man as a unique creation of God.

The phrase *image of God* provides a clue to the meaning of the sanctity of life. The image of God in man is a spiritual reality, because God is a spirit. However, precisely what this image is in relation to the makeup of man is a matter of debate. Some identify it with the threefold view of man: body, soul, and spirit. Others identify it with personality as manifested in intellect, sensibility, and will.

Consequently, the sanctity of life is seen in a man's identity with God, and it involves man in much more than the mere temporal expression of his being—physical life. Because of this identity, in Genesis 9:6 the assault upon another man's physical life is deemed an assault upon God Himself.[12]

At this particular point, the fallacy of the alleged degradation of life by capital punishment becomes apparent. To some abolitionists, the taking of the murderer's life is regarded as a contradiction of the sacredness of his life. Or, to put it another way, the very reason capital punishment was instituted is seen by them as the reason it should be opposed. The error lies in the definition of the sanctity of life. The abolitionist's reluctance at taking the life of the murderer is the result of a perverted sense of values, a failure to recognize the distinction between an individual's physical life and life in the sense of the "image of God." For man is far more than just an animal whose physical breath is his only claim to existence. Man is an eternal spirit, sharing, by virtue of his creation, in the life and being of God Himself. Though this image is marred by original sin, it still exists; though it may be without its original capacities, through regeneration it may again be restored to its fullness. To the humanist, only the physical life is of consequence.

Capital punishment is not a violation of the image of God, because when the image of God is "violated" it is

12. See John Calvin, *Commentary on Genesis* (Grand Rapids: Eerdmans, 1948), 1:295-96, who says, "No one can be injurious to his brother without wounding God Himself."

done so in malice; the murderer seeks to destroy his victim; he seeks to put an end to the *person,* and the best way he knows is to take that person's physical life. Was it not Jesus Himself who said that murder lies in the individual's mind, not in the mere act of killing? (Matt. 5:22). It is out of a full realization of the sanctity of life in terms of the image of God that the call for the death penalty comes.

OTHER IMPLICATIONS

The appeal to the image of God is also seen by some as a safeguard against hasty or unjust retribution. As Martin Luther put it, the image of God "is the outstanding reason why He does not want a human being killed on the strength of individual discretion: man is the noblest creature. . . . God wants us to show respect for this image in one another; He does not want us to shed blood in a tyrannical manner."[13] Later provisions in the Pentateuch, such as the cities of refuge for those who had committed manslaughter, indicate that the death penalty had regard for the sanctity of life.

Within the context of Genesis 9:6, there is the intention to protect life in at least two ways: (1) men in relation to animals, where an animal that kills a man is to be put to death (Gen. 9:2, 5); and (2) man in relation to man, where a man who has killed another man must himself be killed, the idea of deterrence (Gen. 9:5-6). In reference to the first way, the fear instilled into animals is a provision itself for the protection of man's life.

According to 1 Timothy 2:2, civil government exists for the protection of life. The sanctity of life undergirds this divine institution into whose hands is delegated the punishment of death. The degree to which a nation success-

13. Martin Luther, "Lectures on Genesis," in *The Works of Martin Luther* (Philadelphia: Muhlenberg, 1931), 2:141.

fully carries out its divine function can be measured in terms of its recognition of the sanctity of life.

Sanctity of life and justice go hand in hand. For example, in early Germanic law it was possible to provide a token expiation *(Wergild)* for the crime of murder. But through the influence of the Christian church, the death of a man came to be regarded as so grave an offense that it could only be expiated by the death of his killer. The recognition of man's personal worth accounts for the change toward a more severe penalty than was provided for in Germanic law.

Strictly speaking, it is the sanctity of life that tells man murder is terrible and that something should be done about it. Justice, however, tells man *what* must be done about it.

Conclusion

Retributive punishment has its basis in a divine standard of justice as set forth in the Scriptures. Punishment has only one primary purpose, retribution, whereas other purposes such as rehabilitation and deterrence are secondary. In fact, it might be more accurate to refer to punishment as only retributive and rehabilitation as corrective, keeping the two concepts entirely separate. Just retribution is based on a concept of man that recognizes his dignity and ability to make choices and his responsibility for those choices. Finally, the concept of retributive punishment is prior to the demonstration of love, a fact clearly illustrated by the cross. Love can be shown to the condemned murderer by offering him God's forgiveness through Christ, not by sparing his life.

10
Deterrence

Deterrence of murder is usually the basis today of arguments both for and against the death penalty. Those who argue for the retention of the death penalty contend that it does prevent many from committing murder, whereas those who favor the abolition of capital punishment argue that it does not actually deter murder or that it is no better a deterrent, at least, than the prospect of life imprisonment. Both sides produce statistics to support their opposing views.

The subject of deterrence is included at this point following the discussions of justice and retribution, because it is secondary to them as a purpose. In my judgment, however, there is evidence both from within Scripture and other sources that it does indeed deter murder. In this chapter we will deal with the proper place of deterrence as an argument for capital punishment, the importance of strict and fair law enforcement in its effectiveness as a deterrent, the value of statistical arguments, the alternative to capital punishment (life imprisonment), and the scriptural basis for believing in deterrence.

THE PROPER PLACE OF DETERRENCE

Deterrence is a secondary purpose of capital punishment. The utilitarian philosophy of law has made deterrence the chief consideration in the modern debate. Sometimes this form of humanitarianism has been identified with Christianity, so that such a claim as this could be made: "Capital punishment could be justified on Christian grounds only if there were real evidence that it acted as a deterrent."[1] This idea, of course, overlooks most of what the Bible says on the subject.

If it were possible to prove conclusively that capital punishment does not deter murder, the need for capital punishment would remain on a biblical basis. Utilitarians have rejected the biblical basis as not worthy of consideration because it is "obsolete." With only the utilitarian purpose of deterrence remaining, it is not surprising that they have concentrated so much effort into demonstrating that it does not exist to a sufficient degree to warrant the death penalty. But if retribution is the primary purpose for the death penalty, such a punishment is morally justified apart from the issue of deterrence. Deterrence is important, but it is secondary.

THE PROS AND CONS OF DETERRENCE

When it comes to trying to prove that the death penalty indeed deters murder, both proponents and abolitionists turn to statistics for their evidence. These statistics are ordinarily gathered from the United States Census Bureau, and they include both justifiable and excusable homicides, as well as all degrees of murder. These figures have been compared to the less comprehensive murder figures given in *Uniform Crime Reports*, com-

---

1. Robert Meyners, "Two Chairs at San Quentin," *Christian Century* 82 (16 March 1960): 316.

piled by the United States Department of Justice; murder conviction rates given in *Judicial Criminal Statistics;* and murder commitment rates from the publication *Prisoners in State and Federal Prisons and Reformatories,* compiled also by the Bureau of the Census. Such comparisons have revealed a close correspondence, geographically and temporally, to the homicide figures collected by the census bureau, so that the objection that all kinds of homicides are included in the statistics loses some of its force.[2]

The opponents to the death penalty conclude that in the American system of justice, the death penalty is not a significant deterrent. Thus writes Karl F. Schuessler of Indiana University in the November 1952 issue of the *Annals of the American Academy of Political and Social Science:*

> Statistical findings and case studies converge to disprove the claim that the death penalty has any special deterrent value. The belief in the death penalty as a deterrent is repudiated by statistical studies, since they consistently demonstrate that differences in homicide rates are in no way correlated with differences in the use of the death penalty.[3]

To a large extent, the statistics to which Schuessler refers are those gathered and studied by Thorsten Sellin, professor of sociology at the University of Pennsylvania and editor of the *Annals* referred to above.[4]

The Royal Commission on Capital Punishment (1949-

2. William J. Chambliss, *Crime and the Legal Process* (New York: McGraw Hill, 1969), p. 380.

3. Quoted by Donald R. Champion, "Trend Toward Abolition," in *Capital Punishment* (The Royal Commission on Capital Punishment, 1949-53), ed. Grant S. McClellan (New York: H. W. Wilson, 1961), p. 92.

4. Thorsten Sellin, *The Death Penalty* (Philadelphia: American Law Institute, 1959), pp. 19-24, 62-63.

53) of the British Parliament asked Sellin four questions, which are pertinent to the conclusion that should be made on his statistical evidence. The conversation is quoted here at length:

> "We cannot conclude from your statistics . . . that capital punishment has no deterrent effect?"
>
> "No, there is no such conclusion."
>
> "But can we not conclude that if it has a deterrent effect it must be rather small?"
>
> "I can make no such conclusion, because I can find no answer one way or another in these data. . . . It is impossible to draw any inferences from the material that is in my possession, that there is any relationship . . . between a large number of executions, small number of executions, continuous executions, no executions, and what happens to the murder rates."
>
> "I think you have already agreed that capital punishment cannot, on the basis of your figures, be exercising an overwhelming deterrent effect?"
>
> "That is correct."
>
> "But you would not like to go any further than that?"
>
> "No."[5]

The Royal Commission then concludes: "We recognize that it is impossible to arrive confidently at firm conclusions about the deterrent effect of the death penalty, or indeed of any form of punishment."[6]

Sellin's statistics need also to be evaluated in relation to the circumstances under which the death penalty has been inflicted. Long, legal procedures and the possibility of escaping the death penalty as the result of a clever defense would obviously reduce its effectiveness as a deterrent. So argued the *Minority Report* of the Special Commission that investigated the abolition of capital

5. "Function of Capital Punishment," in *Capital Punishment,* p. 71.
6. Ibid.

punishment for the Commonwealth of Massachusetts in 1958.[7]

We observed earlier that the statistics Sellin used contained figures for *all* kinds of homicide, not just those for first-degree murder, which is usually the only form punishable by death. How important a factor is this to the reliability of conclusions made from them? Hugo A. Bedau, a recognized authority and author of what has become one of the standard works on capital punishment, believes that it is significant. He writes:

> All the studies reprinted here are unreliable at the crucial point: is the death penalty an effective deterrent for those kinds of homicides punishable by death? Here is one kind of difficulty that arises when one expects homicide statistics to provide a conclusive answer to this question. Data reported below in Professor Sellin's article shows that the ten year average of annual homicide rates in Ohio fell during the 1920's from 7.9 per 100,000 of population to 3.8 in the 1950's. Yet if the death penalty had been abolished in Ohio at the beginning of this period and if (let us suppose) abolition had been followed by a dozen or so more murders each year thereafter, the general homicide rate would have decreased almost exactly as in fact it has, and at no time would the rate for any given year be more than a tenth of one per cent greater than it has been. Thus, while we could truthfully say that the abolition of the death penalty in Ohio had been followed by a decrease in the general homicide rate, it would also have been true that abolition resulted in an *increase* in the total number of murders, and this despite the constancy of the ratio of total homicides to murders (except in the first year after abolition). For all we know, this is exactly what has happened in all the abolition states, which without exception show a steadily declining general homicide rate over the past several decades. The number of crimes at stake here

7. Reprinted in *Capital Punishment*, pp. 76-77.

is so small that they would never be noticed by anyone who relies on the ordinary vital and criminal statistics of homicide.[8]

Since the work of Sellin in the 1950s the moratorium and Supreme Court ruling have provided a new set of circumstances out of which a new set of statistics can be drawn. Advocates of the death penalty consider these newer statistics to be more reliable than those used by Thorsten Sellin.

Writers like Frank G. Carrington call attention to the fact that since the virtual cessation of actual executions murders have more than doubled.[9] Such statistics look like this[10]:

Year	Executions	Murders
1957	65	8,060
1958	49	8,220
1959	49	8,580
1960	56	9,140
1961	42	8,600
1962	47	8,400
1963	21	8,500
1964	15	9,250
1965	7	9,850
1966	1	10,920
1967	2	12,090
1968	0	13,590
1969	0	14,590
1970	0	15,810
1971	0	17,630

8. Hugo Adam Bedau, ed., *The Death Penalty in America* (New York: Anchor Books, 1964), pp. 265-66.
9. Frank G. Carrington, *Neither Cruel nor Unusual* (Arlington House: New Rochelle, 1978), p. 54.
10. Cited by Karl Spence, "Crime and Punishment," in *National Review* 35 (16 September 1983):1140 ff.

1972	0	18,520
1973	0	19,510
1974	0	20,600
1975	0	20,510
1976	0	18,780
1977	1	19,120
1978	0	19,560
1979	2	21,460
1980	0	23,040
1981	1	22,520

These statistics are subject to the criticism that they fail to take into account the increase in population in the United States during those years, but they are superior to Sellin's in that they compare only murders to executions, although it is not clear if the murder figures include the kinds of homicides not punishable by death.

Another kind of statistic such as is published in the annual *Uniform Crime Reports* may be more valid, since they avoid the criticism of failing to account for population growth. Beginning with 1966, the year the moratorium took place, the following figures provide a similar picture:

Year	Murders per 100,000 population
1966	5.6
1967	6.1
1968	6.8
1969	7.2
1970	7.8
1971	8.5
1972	8.9
1973	9.3
1974	9.7
1975	9.6

1976	8.8
1977	8.8
1978	9
1979	10
1980	10
1981	10
1982	9

Between 1966 and 1982, the murder *rate* has also doubled, and the rate of increase has been fairly close to the previous table.

Apart from the issue of statistics, there are evidences that capital punishment is a deterrent. For example, the Los Angeles Police Department filed a report with the California Senate Judiciary Committee in February 1960, which showed thirteen robbery suspects admitted that they had used toy guns, empty guns, or simulated guns in robberies in order to avoid a killing and getting the gas chamber.[11] Though some of these confessions may have been made in order to impress the police, they cannot be entirely discounted.

Later in 1970 and 1971 a study was made by the Los Angeles Police Department of ninety-nine persons who explained why they went unarmed during their crimes[12]:

1. Deterred by fear of death penalty from carrying a real weapon or any weapon at all—fifty
2. Unaffected by death penalty because it was no longer being enforced—seven
3. Undeterred by death penalty; would kill whether it was enforced or not—ten
4. Unaffected by death penalty, because they would have not carried a weapon in any event for various reasons—thirty-two

11. Quoted in Bedau, p. 167.
12. Cited by Carrington, from the brief of the State of California in Aikens vs. California, No. 68-5027, October term, 1971, U.S. Supreme Court.

During this time, the death penalty was on the statute books in California.

There are weaknesses in the arguments abolitionists use in interpreting their own evidences. For example, statistics reveal that over one-half of murders are crimes of passion during which no deterrent could have been effective. The conclusion is that the death penalty should be abolished for murder, since it is not preventing it. The Canadian Parliamentary Committee that studied Sellin's statistical researches disagreed with this interpretation. They instead concluded:

> This would seem to demonstrate that the death penalty, coupled with the excellent standards of law enforcement prevailing in Canada, has been successful in deterring the commission of deliberate, premeditated murders and reducing their incidence to minimum proportions. The deterrent effect may also be indicated by the widespread association of the crime of murder with the death penalty which is undoubtedly one reason why murder is regarded as such a grave and abhorrent crime.[13]

Similarly, the assumption that none of the men on death row ever thought of the death penalty[14] must be coupled with the assumption that men *not* on death row (because they did not commit any capital crime) do not think of the death penalty either. Such, of course, cannot be proved one way or the other. The opinions of men on death row "probably have almost no relevance one way or the other on the question of deterrence."[15]

The deterrent value of capital punishment must be balanced with the fact that there are other kinds of deterrents in addition to it, such as cultural and religious factors, which would complement the death penalty as a

---

13 Quoted in Bedau, p. 268.
14 Such is the testimony of many. See Chambliss, pp. 387-88 for quoted example from Lewis E. Lawes.
15 Bedau, p. 270.

deterrent and whose presence would be necessary for its full effectiveness. These factors are believed by some authorities to have a definite bearing upon the statistics on homicide as they relate to various parts of the country.[16] To admit this does not necessarily diminish the value or necessity of capital punishment; it may only point up the fact that some extreme form of punishment is needed for people who are the least deterred by these cultural or religious factors. Not only the current lack of executions but the growing permissiveness of our society must affect the rate of murders. If there is any validity to the statistics cited above, it is due to the lack of enforcement of the death penalty plus these other factors.

THE ALTERNATIVE TO CAPITAL PUNISHMENT

The alternative to capital punishment is life imprisonment. Cesare Beccaria was an early exponent of life imprisonment instead of the death penalty. He spoke of the "continual example of a man deprived of his liberty, condemned, as a beast of burden, to repair, by his labour, the injury he has done to society."[17] Though Beccaria's "perpetual slavery" might indeed possess significant deterrent effect, such a concept is a far cry from modern penal standards, especially where parole is possible even to murderers after a few years of imprisonment.

Bedau calls attention to the fact that we know that every year about 6 in every 100,000 of the population (it is higher at present) are not deterred from murder by the death penalty. "What we want to know is whether half a dozen, or a dozen, or hundreds or thousands are deterred by it, who wouldn't be deterred by the threat of a prison sentence."[18] This is called "differential deter-

16. Ibid., p. 262.
17. Cesare Beccaria, "On Crime and Punishment," in *An Essay on Crimes and Punishments,* trans. E. D. Ingraham (Stanford: Academic Reprints, 1952), p. 99.
18. Bedau, p. 261.

rence," and no social scientist has directly studied this question. It may be impossible to do so directly.

Life imprisonment is regarded by opponents to the death penalty as a more attractive form of punishment, because it seems less brutal, carries the possibility for rehabilitation, and can always be reversed if further evidence indicates the victim's innocence. However, such punishment does not meet the strict requirements of justice from the biblical standpoint. If the Bible indeed has the proper insight into this issue, are there any possible reasons why life imprisonment might be far from the best interests of the convict?

From a spiritual standpoint, life imprisonment may not be conducive to repentance in all cases. Unless a punishment is "just," the criminal may not be as likely to recognize the seriousness of his crime and repent. From this perspective, life imprisonment could be a grave *injustice* to the murderer.

Furthermore, some, including criminals, regard extended incarceration as worse than death, for their standard of life is so seriously altered by it as to make the thought of a life without liberty unbearable. This very fact may be a clue to the possibility that in reality, life imprisonment *exceeds* the requirements of retribution. Such a viewpoint is obviously not shared by many men facing the two alternatives of life imprisonment or death. Most human beings have come to regard death as final and even mere animal existence as preferable. The question is, does life imprisonment not actually rob a man of his dignity as a human being?

This consideration has seldom figured into discussions of the alternative of life imprisonment, probably because there is, in most cases, no such thing as a literal life's sentence. After about fourteen years of imprisonment, parole is available to many murderers whom experts deem as rehabilitated. In the final analysis, therefore, the debate over life imprisonment versus capital punishment is rather academic under the present system.

The factor of deterrence is extremely difficult, if not impossible, to prove, because only the failures of the death penalty to deter murder show up in statistics. In addition to this, other factors deter murder, and interrelation of all factors cannot scientifically be known.

Biblical revelation, which will be considered next, supplies evidence that the death penalty is a deterrent. Many peoples' personal experience and innermost feelings tell them that the fear of death prevents murder. In a sense, the belief in capital punishment as a deterrent is an article of faith. But if deterrence is not the primary purpose for capital punishment, the issue should be allowed to rest here.

The Scriptural Basis for Deterrence

There is ample biblical evidence that capital punishment has a deterrent effect. Some are ignorant of this fact and believe that the concept of deterrence is a development subsequent to biblical times.

Deterrence by punishment in general is seen clearly in Ecclesiastes 8:11: "Because the sentence against an evil deed is not executed quickly, therefore the hearts of the sons of men among them are given fully to do evil." Here the thought involves both the enforcement of law and the fact of law as factors in deterrence.

Deterrence by the death penalty is specifically found in Deuteronomy 17:12-13, where presumption before a priest is to be punished by death to "purge the evil from Israel" (expiation or retribution) so that "all the people will hear and be afraid, and will not act presumptuously again" (deterrence).

In Deuteronomy 19:15-21, a proved false witness in any case was to be punished in the same way as the person against whom he bore false witness would have been punished. Again, both the expiatory purpose, "Thus you shall purge the evil from among you," and the deterrence purpose, "And the rest will hear and be afraid, and will never again do such an evil thing among you," are mentioned.

Deuteronomy 21:18-21 mentions the "stubborn and rebellious son" who resists the efforts of his parents to correct him and who is to be presented to the elders of the city; upon clear evidence, he is to be stoned by all the men of the city in order to "remove the evil from your midst, and all Israel shall hear of it and fear."

The idea of deterrence is explicit in Romans 13:3-4: "For rulers are not a cause of fear for good behavior, but for evil. Do you want to have no fear of authority? Do what is good, and you will have praise from the same." In this passage both the retributive and deterrence purposes appear, but the important feature in relation to deterrence is that the function of government in keeping law and order *depends* on deterrence in two forms: (1) actual restraint by force, when necessary (and this obviously involves the sword as a tool of prevention as well as capital punishment) and (2) fear of punishment up to the death penalty.

It appears that the scriptural concept of deterrence is based upon the principle of human responsibility, the implication that most crime is committed by those who are capable of rational decisions for which they can be held accountable. This runs counter to much recent psychology. If modern thinking predominates, we will witness the gradual eroding of the deterrence factor in punishment for all forms of crime.

In Conclusion—Is the Risk Worth It?

Having considered the various purposes of capital punishment, we arrive at a final problem: Is the risk of executing innocent people worth capital punishment? The possibility of human error becomes a determining factor in the question of capital punishment—especially to those who do not recognize the divine mandate, the necessity of the power of life and death for human government to function in a sinful world, and the priority of justice. One's scale of values ultimately determines his answer to the question of the necessity for capital punishment. If one's concept of values is biblical, he will see the necessity of capital punishment regardless of the possibility of human error.

The question of human error, however, usually is grossly exaggerated. The number of those conclusively proved to have been wrongly executed is extremely small. Furthermore, the argument is not applicable in cases where guilt is conclusive. Therefore, the argument is that a law should not be in existence because an extremely few cases of injustice have occurred. The answer, in the light of this, is even more clear than before: reform the judicial procedure; do not abolish the law that is suffering abuse. This, too, is the answer in those cases where it is alleged that there are more blacks and poor people executed than whites and wealthy individuals, who may be able to afford better lawyers.

It is significant that Scripture assumes the capability of man to make judgment in capital cases. The various scriptural safeguards, such as the cities of refuge and the requirement of at least two witnesses (Num. 35), suggest that, if man proceeded cautiously within the framework of reverence for life and concern for justice, his decisions would be right and just.

The possibility exists, however, that human beings will make mistakes. Any sort of punishment carries the risk of injustice, but punishment as such cannot be discredited. The risk of failure does not reflect upon the morality of punishment.

Some claim that it would be better for a guilty man to go free than for an innocent man to die. Such an ethic must assume that the failure to apply justice is better than the misapplication of justice. Must we be faced with a choice of equal evil over against equal injustice? Unpunished guilt is precisely the same species of evil as punished innocence. Their claim also assumes that the punishment of the guilty is not as important as the immunity of the innocent. The choice, however, is not an either/or between immunity and punishment, as the ethic implies, for justice requires *both*.

The force of the argument is not lessened by the fact that opponents of capital punishment are advocating life imprisonment, not total freedom from punishment, as the preceding paragraph may seem to imply. The issue is that anything less than death is not the full measure of punishment required by justice; thus, anything less than death is an injustice. The question must be settled, therefore, as to whether the death penalty is just, not as to whether lack of punishment is better than punishing the wrong person. The latter question really is irrelevant.

Part 4
The Problem
of Progressive Revelation

11
The Meaning of Progressive Revelation

One of the most elusive arguments against capital punishment is the one that claims the spirit and teaching of the New Testament in some way or other abrogates the institution of capital punishment. This argument, however stated, involves a principle called "progressive revelation," which is recognized by all Bible scholars who accept the evangelical concept of revelation. It is the question of whether the later revelation, the New Testament, has substantially altered former revelation, that which is to be found in the Old Testament.

DEFINITION

Revelation is the communication of truth from God to man. *Progressive* revelation is the gradual unfolding of this truth in the Bible. No single truth in the Bible first appeared in its fullest development; rather, it appeared in its simplest form, and, as a rivulet gains in quantity and force as other tiny streams join it, developing first into a stream and becoming eventually a great river, truth consumates later in Scripture in its full-orbed significance. John Calvin described this phenomenon as a process in which "as the day of full revelation approached with the passing of time, the more he increased each day the brightness of its manifestation."[1] God's revelation as we have it in the Bible was not given in one single act. It was gradually unfolded in a series of acts and communications, which entered the experience of man through historical acts, encounters, and personal revelations.

The plan of salvation is one of the clearest examples of this process. In Genesis 3:15 is found the "seed text" of the gospel. This is the promise immediately following the Fall of man that the seed of the woman should bruise the serpent's head, the promise of the coming of Christ to deliver sinners from the power of Satan. Further development of this theme appears in the covenant with Abraham (Gen. 12:3) where the patriarch is promised that in him—that is, his seed—would all the families of the earth be blessed. Paul the apostle makes clear that this seed referred to Jesus Christ (Gal. 3:16). Further revelation concerning the mechanics of salvation is found in the institution of sacrifices in Exodus and Leviticus, which pointed to the sacrifice of Jesus Christ on the cross as the Lamb of God. In the prophets we have further revelation regarding the Person of the coming Redeemer and the manner of His birth. For example, Isaiah 7:14 declares the truth that He would be born of a virgin and would be called "Immanuel," or "God with us." Later, Isaiah was the one through whom was given the idea of the suffering Messiah who would bear the sins of the world. These texts and many others contributed to a rather complete picture of Jesus Christ, so that the writers of the gospels were able to quote the revelation already

---

1. John Calvin, *Institutes of the Christian Religion,* ed. John T. McNeill, trans. Ford L. Battles (Philadelphia: Westminster, 1965), 1:446-47.

given concerning Him by way of confirmation of His credentials as the Son of God. Indeed, the revelation had become so detailed and adequate, that the apostles and disciples of Christ were able to present the gospel to the world from the pages of the Old Testament, especially to the Jews, before the first gospel had been penned (Acts 18:25). The progressive unfolding of the truth revealed in Jesus Christ had reached an amazing fullness by the time Jesus had begun His ministry.

PRINCIPLES OF PROGRESSIVE REVELATION

PROGRESSIVE REVELATION INVOLVES NEWLY REVEALED TRUTH

Progressive revelation enters into sound interpretation of the Bible. It is not only important that God, through human instrumentality, has revealed certain truths, but it is likewise essential that the interpreter of the Bible be aware of its progressive nature.

The progress of revelation gradually introduces features that enhance and complement a given theme, and, when the last feature has been introduced, the reader possesses a complete knowledge, which has not been contradicted at any point and which is dependent upon the combined contribution of all the successive additions for an accurate understanding of the theme. The importance of the recognition of progressive revelation, then, is seen in the fact that no final word can be said about any doctrine at any point along the way, but the complete statement, in order to be accurate, must involve the total teaching of the Bible.

The principle of the progress of revelation operates in the case of all biblical themes, of which capital punishment is one. No one would be willing to admit that Genesis 9:6 contains the sum total of the teaching on capital punishment. What the Mosaic law has to say makes its contribution. Genesis 9:6 mentions no exceptions to capital punishment. Further revelation, as the principle of progressive revelation demands, gives the interpreter further light on the teaching.

Progressive revelation is not only important in terms of what is *added* to a theme over a period of time but in terms of what is sometimes *modified* and even *superseded*. This is the crux of the problem with which the succeeding chapters will deal. The problem may be stated in the form of a question: Has further revelation so affected the law of capital punishment that it should be abolished?

When something is superseded, that superseding is done so by something that is superior. For example, the system of sacrifices, which was an interim provision pending the ultimate sacrifice of Christ, was obviously superseded by Christ's sacrifice when it came about (Heb. 9:1—10:18). In other words, Christians no longer make animal sacrifices as those in Israel were once required to do, but simply ask for forgiveness on the basis of the completed sacrifice of Christ when they confess their sins (1 John 1:9). Nothing is *contradicted* in the sacrificial system in the sense that it is said to have been wrong. It served its function and pointed to Christ. The better sacrifice of Christ has superseded it now, and the old system has been done away. Its value does not cease, though, for through its foreshadowings of that perfect and complete sacrifice in Jesus Christ, the interpreter can better understand the meaning of the perfect sacrifice. Thus, as a part of progressive revelation it makes its contribution to the doctrine of the atonement. Therefore, in reference to capital punishment, the question should be stated in this way: Has anything been revealed in the New Testament that by its superior nature supersedes the institution of capital punishment? We will consider this question next.

There are several issues or themes in the New Testament that some claim to have had such an effect on capital punishment as to supersede it. These teachings are: (1) the so-called abolition of the law of Moses, (2) Christ's teaching on forgiveness, and (3) the expiatory, or propitiatory, character of Christ's death. In the next few chapters we will deal with these themes in that order.

12
The Question of the Abolition of the Law

Many of the arguments against capital punishment come from those who accept the authority of the Bible. Few of them deny that the death penalty was commanded under the law of Moses. In order to escape the implications of this clear mandate, they must argue that this mandate has been done away as a part of the Mosaic law, which they claim has been abolished in Jesus Christ.

Some argue against what they call the legalistic application of Old Testament texts to justify capital punishment. In order to be consistent, they declare, it would be necessary to follow everything else in the law. They believe that it is inconsistent to argue for the literal observation of the death penalty in the case of murder and ignore it for the several other crimes such as adultery, which are also capital crimes under the Mosaic law. It is better, they suggest, to recognize that the New Testament cancels the prescriptions of the law. Strictly speaking, however, Genesis 9:6 *antedates* the law of Moses. It is possible to include this original institution as part of the system that was allegedly abolished, or is this feature of the Mosaic law something that has an enduring quality like the moral commandments? In other words, does the Bible still command the death penalty, or has it gone out like the practice of animal sacrifices?

The big question is, has the law been abolished? This may be an inaccurate and misleading word. When this word is used, as in Ephesians 2:15, it involves the Greek verb *luo* which means "destroy" and implies a total removal of the law in the sense that it was a barrier between Jews and Gentiles. Actually, Jesus clearly said that He had not come to "abolish" (stronger form of *luo*—*kataluo*) the law (Matt. 5:17).

Definition of "Law"

The word *law* is used several ways in the Bible. It can refer, for example, to what has been called inherent or intrinsic law, that which God required of every creature because of His own character. This law was binding upon all men from Adam to Moses (Gen. 26:5; Rom. 2:14-15; 5:12-14) and is still the basis for the accountability of the Gentile world, which is without the Scriptures (Rom. 2:14-15). Sometimes the word *law* refers to the law of human government (1 Tim. 1:8-10). At other times it may mean the revealed will of God in any form (cf. its usage in Rom. 7:15-25 and 8:4). Finally, *law* can be used in reference to the law of Christ (1 Cor. 9:20-21) though the "commandments of Christ" may refer to *both* Old Testament and New Testament commandments as Jesus reinterpreted and reapplied them.

The law of Moses, or the Mosaic covenant, was given to Israel as a system of government while they were in the land of Palestine. It was a law prescribed as their rule of life, suited to the times and the conditions of their national existence. When these conditions ceased to exist at their dispersion, the law actually could not be kept literally (e.g., the requirements for pilgrimages to Jerusalem). These factors alone should give the interpreter pause in any attempt to impose the law of Moses in an unqualified way upon anyone today.

Some, in their efforts to preserve some parts of the law of Moses so that they can be applied today—and this would include capital punishment—have argued that the law must be viewed as consisting of at least two parts, moral and ceremonial, and that the moral, by its very nature, is binding upon men today. The problem in making this distinction, however, is that the Ten Commandments, though they contain obvious universal principles, are beset with an inherent obsolescence. This does not pertain to the archaic language in which they are couched. It refers, for example, to the fourth commandment, which, if it were consistently applied as the children of Israel were told, would involve regulations that would be thoroughly impractical. Now it might be argued by these same people that these regulations are not part of the enduring moral ethic contained in the Decalogue. But then neither is the death penalty, which is a part of the civil legislation.

It is true that the law of Moses had its divisions. There were the "commandments," governing the civil life (Ex. 21:1—24:11) and the "ordinances," pertaining to the religious life (Ex. 24:12—31:18). However, no such distinctions were made by the writers of the New Testament when they declared that the condemnation of the law was done away by Christ. Bible scholars who have dealt with the use of the term *law*, when reference is to the Christian's freedom from its penalty, agree that the writers had no such distinction in mind but rather were referring to the law of Moses—the commandments, judgments, and ordinances—as a unit. In Gerhard Kittel's *Theological Dictionary of the New Testament* it is claimed that the term *law* usually applies to the whole

Pentateuch when it appears in the gospels,[1] whereas Paul makes "no distinction between the Decalogue and the rest of the legal material in the Old Testament."[2]

Several points regarding the definition of the law of Moses should be borne in mind. First, it was the rule of life given to a particular people, Israel. Second, it served to govern them in every area of life while they were in the Promised Land. Third, though it had divisions, it was regarded by Israel and the writers of the New Testament as a unit. Therefore, any attempt to preserve a part of it for application today in order to preserve capital punishment is complicated with difficulties and inconsistencies. But by the same token, no sweeping generalizations can be tolerated to the effect that the abolition of the law of Moses is stretched to include anything that does not fit into one's scheme in the words "The New Testament modifies the Old Testament." When the New Testament writers used the word *law*, they had the law of Moses in mind sometimes and at other times the whole Pentateuch.

MEANING OF THE ABOLITION OF THE LAW

Even a brief examination of the New Testament, especially the Acts and epistles, will leave the reader with the impression that something has changed regarding the law of Moses. The Christian's relationship to the law is not the same as was the Israelite's. However, it is also obvious that many things contained in the law appear also in the New Testament.

What is the relationship of the Christian to the Law? There are four aspects to this new relationship, and none of them will have any bearing on the validity of capital

1. *Theological Dictionary of the New Testament,* ed. Gerhard Kittel, trans. Geoffrey Bromiley (Grand Rapids: Eerdmans, 1964-68), s.v. Νόμος [nomos].
2. Ibid.

punishment: (1) specific parts of the Law of Moses have been suspended as an obligation of the Christian, (2) legalistic applications of Mosaic law are not valid to the Christian, (3) the penalty or condemnation has been removed for the Christian, and (4) the Mosaic law has been fulfilled for the believer by the obedience of Christ.

SPECIFIC PARTS OF MOSAIC LAW HAVE BEEN SUSPENDED

Some dispensationalists like to think of a new economy with a new set of binding regulations and the Mosaic code abolished as a unit. This may have some merit as a concept, but its liability is in its tendency to encourage some dispensationalists to ignore vast areas of Old Testament civil and social legislation in their construction of a Christian ethical system, even, in some cases, a serious study of the Ten Commandments. All of this, of course, flies in the face of the fact that *all* Scripture is "profitable" (2 Tim. 3:16-17).

Against this tendency, which is to be seen in the whole spectrum of theological systems, are a few New Testament passages that seem to validate a legitimate use of the law by New Testament believers, for example 1 Timothy 1:8: "But we know that the Law is good, if one uses it lawfully," and Jesus' words in Matthew 5:17, "Do not think I came to abolish the Law or the Prophets; I did not come to abolish, but to fulfill."

Besides this, if one carefully examines the use of the Old Testament by New Testament writers, he will discover that they used it frequently as though it had some direct bearing on a point they were making: "For it is written in the Law of Moses, 'You shall not muzzle the ox while he is threshing'! God is not concerned about oxen, is He? Or is He speaking altogether for our sake? Yes, for our sake it was written. . . . If we sowed spiritual things in you, is it too much if we should reap material things from you?" Obviously, Paul knew how to glean the principle from the law before he made the application, but this illustrates the fact that when he stated in 2 Timothy, "All Scripture . . . is profitable," he considered the law of Moses to be included.

There are, on the other side of the issue, some specific items in Moses that have been removed from obligation for one reason or another. One is the observance of the seventh day of the week, although some might argue for the principle of a Sabbath for today (see Rom. 14:5). Others include the ceremonial portions of the law due to their relation to the death and priesthood of Christ (Heb. 10:1-2).

On what basis can one make the distinction between what is valid and what is not valid for today? Simply from explicit statements as just illustrated. It is not valid, however, to argue for a wholesale abolition of Mosaic law from such passages as "you are not under law, but under grace" (Rom. 6:14) and thereby grossly violate the context where "under law" means under the *condemnation* of law.

The sum of it is that Christians today must use all of God's Word as valid by applying a grammatical, historical interpretation to it before applying it to themselves. This includes pre-Mosaic, Mosaic, and even New Testament sections addressed to the church. In the latter case, both dispensationalists and non-dispensationalists recognize historical and cultural elements in commandments given to first-century believers as they seek to discover the enduring, trans-cultural principles to be applied to their lives. For example, how should one interpret and apply the matters in 1 Corinthians 8 about eating meat offered to idols? The first step is to understand thoroughly what it meant to Paul's readers and then look for the principle. The principle that emerges is tolerance for one another in matters of personal conscience. The law must be handled in the same manner, with no foregone conclusions about whether it is for believers today, except in cases where the New Testament specifically states it is not (see, for another example, Acts 15).

THE LAW MUST NOT BE LEGALISTICALLY APPLIED

Some of the New Testament passages used to prove that the law of Moses is abolished are actually statements against its misuse. Most of the misuse of the law involves efforts to keep it for the purpose of gaining salvation or greater merit from God. Laws themselves are not wrong to the Christian, but his application of the law to gain initial or continued approval from God is "legalism." Being obedient to Christ, which is taught throughout the New Testament, arises properly out of love and gratitude, and it involves "keeping commandments."

Thus the Galatians' efforts to be circumcised according to the law of Moses was condemned by Paul, not because circumcision was wrong in itself (most Gentile baby boys today in America are circumcised) but because they were seeking to maintain their justification by doing it (Gal. 3:1-11). Paul allowed for the Jews' continuing observance of the Law so long as it was not a threat to the principle of justification by faith. (Circumcision, incidentally, falls into the category of things that have been removed from obligation like the seventh day of the week.)

THE PENALTY OR CONDEMNATION OF LAW HAS BEEN REMOVED

Paul refers to the penalty of the law as a "curse" in Galatians 3:13: "Christ redeemed us from the curse of the Law, having become a curse for us." This penalty, which is the result of disobedience to the law (Lev. 26:14-20; Deut. 11:26-32; 27:26), is pronounced upon all men, because all have disobeyed (Rom. 3:23). Strictly speaking, of course, the penalty of the Mosaic law was upon those who were bound by the law, that is, Israel (the possible meaning of Rom. 3:19-20). Those to whom the law was not given, Gentiles, are judged by inherent law (Rom. 2:12-16). The end result is the same.

This penalty has been abolished or removed by the perfect obedience and sacrifice of Christ (Gal. 3:13), so that the believer is free to present himself to another Master (Rom. 6:15-23). Paul describes the former situation under law as being in obedience to sin, for the law, due to the weakness of the flesh, was unable to produce righteous obedience in its subjects, and the result was sin (Rom. 8:3). While this penalty existed, the one under law was not free. Servitude to Christ, however, cannot be so described, for it is voluntary (Rom. 6:13), and the believer may, for a time at least, place himself under the law again by imposing its ordinances upon himself legalistically (Gal. 3:10-14).

The penalty of the law is death (Rom. 6:23). In the final analysis, this means separation from God (Eph. 2:1; Col. 2:13), but physical death is one of the inevitable results of the original sin of Adam (Rom. 5:12). In removing this penalty, God has granted eternal life to all who believe (John 3:16). Abolition of the penalty of the law brings the believer into the sphere of a resurrected life here and now (Rom. 6:5).

THE LAW HAS BEEN FULFILLED

Jesus stated that He came not to abolish the law but to fulfill it (Matt. 5:17). What did He mean by that?

First of all, Christ interpreted the law of Moses in terms of the inner motives and causes of sin within a man (Matt. 5:22, 28). In Matthew 5:39 and 44 He corrected some of the Jewish traditional interpretations of the law. The *lex talionis,* an eye for an eye and a tooth for a tooth, was not to give one the excuse for personal revenge; instead His people were commanded to love their enemies, an idea not foreign to the Old Testament, as Exodus 23:5 proves: "If you see the donkey of one who hates you lying helpless under its load, you shall refrain from leaving it to him, you shall surely release it with him."

Second, Jesus fulfilled the law in the sense that He kept it fully and perfectly (Heb. 4:15; Gal. 4:4-5). This perfect obedience qualified Him to be the Redeemer of those under the law, for in order to pay the penalty of the law by His death for anyone but Himself, He needed not to be under that penalty Himself.

Third, according to Hebrews 9:11—10:25, Jesus fulfilled the law in even a greater way than has been already suggested: by dying on the cross. The sacrificial system of the Mosaic law not only provided a gracious means of passing over the sins of the nation as well as the individual, but it pointed to the ultimate sacrifice of Jesus, the Lamb of God. The Levitical offerings or sacrifices were, at best, a temporary provision whose efficacy rested on the certainty of the only sacrifice that could really take away sin, that of Jesus Christ. This is a fulfillment of type and antitype, shadow and substance (Heb. 8:4, 5; 10:1).

Further fulfillment of the law by the Lord Jesus Christ is seen in reference to the Levitical priesthood, according to Hebrews 7:11-12. Christ, a priest after the order of Melchizedek, superseded the priesthood after the order of Aaron. The writer to the Hebrews argues that the law of the priesthood must have passed away simply by virtue of the existence of a new priesthood. He then goes on to argue for the superiority of the Melchizedek priesthood, but the thought is that the Aaronic priesthood supplied a need temporarily, which is not permanently supplied by the new priesthood of Jesus Christ.

By His death, Christ has fulfilled the demands of the law for justice for those who place their faith in Him as their sacrifice for sin. This is what is meant by substitutionary atonement (1 Pet. 2:24; 1 Tim. 2:6). In this sense, the law was not ignored, which would have been contrary to the character of God, but was satisfied by the propitiation of Christ (1 John 2:2).

CONCLUSION

In none of the examples of the new relationship of the believer to the law is there a necessary abolition of the death penalty merely because it is part of an antiquated system of the past. The closest Jesus came to doing anything of this kind was in His reinterpretation of the law of retaliation. Yet even here He was dealing with a Pharisaical misuse of it in which they sought to justify personal revenge. When applied to civil legislation, the *lex talionis* is alive and well as a statement both of justice and restraint.

13
The Enduring Nature of Capital Punishment

In defining the meaning of law and its relation to the believer, a basis has now been established for a conclusion about the unique nature of the death penalty. *Law* cannot be understood as meaning the whole of the Old Testament all of the time or merely the formal Mosiac legislation all of the time. Even if the believer's relation to the law has been changed, material prior to the law of Moses is not necessarily affected. Furthermore, we have seen that a careful study of what this means does not necessarily have any bearing on capital punishment. The fact of the law's penalty being removed through Christ is irrelevant also. Neither did Christ's fulfillment of the law have any necessary bearing upon it. Christ's reinterpretation of the law left the death penalty unscathed. In keeping the law so that He might redeem men from its penalty is really the only valid sense in which it can be said that the "law was abolished," and that pertains to its penalty. The sacrifices were fulfilled by Christ, but that had no effect upon capital punishment.

Capital punishment, by its very nature, has not been

affected by the changes Jesus brought relative to the law. This argument is not conclusive, but it at least helps to identify capital punishment as an enduring element like the commandment "You shall not commit adultery" (Ex. 20:14), which is a part of the believer's ethic today. In this chapter we look at (1) the priority of capital punishment and (2) the universality of capital punishment.

PRIORITY OF THE LAW

The mandate of Genesis 9:6 is basically unaffected by any changes in the law of Moses simply by the fact that it existed long before the law. Another reason to believe this is the fact that another pre-Mosaic institution, the convenant with Abraham, is explicitly stated by Paul to continue in its effect despite the giving of the law of Moses. Here is what Paul says:

> Brethren, I speak in terms of human relations: even though it is only a man's covenant, yet when it has been ratified, no one sets it aside or adds conditions to it. Now the promises were spoken to Abraham and to his seed. He does not say, "And to seeds," as referring to many, but rather to one, "And to your seed," that is, Christ. What I am saying is this: the Law, which came four hundred and thirty years later, does not invalidate a covenant previously ratified by God, so as to nullify the promise. (Gal. 3:15-17)

It is true that there is no connection between Genesis 9:6 and the Abrahamic covenant, but the fact remains that something that preceded the law is still in effect simply because of its intrinsic nature and priority. Does this not allow for the possibility that Genesis 9:6 might still remain in force?

UNIVERSALITY OF SCOPE

It is also possible that Genesis 9:6 may be enduring in its nature due to the nature of its need and the nature of the crime that it punishes. Actually, there is no indication in the Bible that the Mosaic law and the covenant with Noah were ever associated. The covenant with Noah was universal in its implications, whereas the law of Moses was limited in its application to Israel alone, at least as it is set forth in Scripture. Many recognize the Noahic covenant as the institution of human government by the command for man himself to undertake the punishment of the gravest of crimes, murder.

The important thing to observe is that Noah and his family stood at the beginning of a new human civilization to which new powers and dominion were given for the first time. This civilization branched out into all the races and nationalities that are known today. Only one of these was Israel, to whom the law was given. The covenant with Noah was with him and his posterity. Much of that posterity lived and died never having heard of the law of Moses but carried into its laws and traditions the basic elements of the covenant with Noah, including the right of man to punish man with death for the crime murder. It is rather ironic that Israel, as it has been noted in the historical survey, may have been among those who least observed this law, even though they possessed the clearest mandate of it in the Old Testament Scriptures.

If further history and further revelation had reduced the occurrence of murder, we might logically expect the punishment for it to have been abolished simply through practice. Such is not the case. Murder remains the most heinous of crimes, and yet there are those who call for the abolition of the penalty of death on the basis of further revelation. If anything, further revelation has taught the Bible student that the causes for murder have not ceased to exist, that man's nature is basically the same and needs to be dealt with by at least the same restraints as God knew it required over six thousand years ago.

14
Forgiveness Versus Capital Punishment

THE ALLEGED CONTRADICTION

Few will deny that the New Testament is characterized by a different emphasis from the Old, especially in regard to God's disposition to forgive. This is not to say that the Old Testament, and specifically the dispensation of the law, was a total stranger to forgiveness. The provision for atonement of sins in the sacrificial system attests to this. The biggest difference between the two dispensations lies, naturally, in the fact that in the New the Son of God Himself was on earth to forgive, and He Himself declined to condemn or judge (John 12:47). It has been alleged by opponents of capital punishment that such punishment is contradicted by this very teaching and mission of Jesus, a mission characterized in such words as "The Son of man came to seek and to save that which was lost" (Luke 19:10) and "I came that they may have life, and may have it abundantly" (John 10:10). Surely, they say, there is no place for capital punishment in a religion that offers life.

Though the approach may vary in reference to the attitude of Christ toward the sinner, these people seem to be talking about Jesus' disposition to forgive. For example, Jesus' repudiation of the *lex talionis* in Matthew 5:38-42 and the apparent abolition of the principle of retribution is used as a proof text against capital punishment. Another text often cited is Romans 12:17-19 where the apostle Paul exhorts Christians not to seek vengeance, as though this applies to civil authorities.

Judging by the way in which some abolitionists of the death penalty speak of forgiveness and especially the Christian's responsibility to forgive, one might suspect that they fail to understand the true nature of forgiveness. Observe the following quotations: Jesus "taught that forgiveness was the greatest of human virtues." No Christian "can advocate capital punishment and be true to his faith."[1]

> We witness to the compassion and forgiveness . . . that God has shown us in Jesus Christ when we allow our hands and passions to be restrained in our dealings with all men and especially with the most despicable.[2]

This last quotation is connected with an argument against capital punishment, not just the Christian's dealings with men personally.

There is a vast difference between human and divine forgiveness in terms of atonement. It is a simple matter for one human being to forgive another, but God's forgiveness for sinful man is complicated and costly, much modern theology notwithstanding. In order for God to

---

1. Julia E. Johnsen, ed., *Capital Punishment* (New York: H. W. Wilson, 1939), p. 83.
2. Nevin E. Kendall, "A Christian View," in *Capital Punishment,* p. 53.

forgive and still remain consistent with His character, He must see that the debt to His holiness, caused by man's offense, is paid—though it is paid by Himself. God must require atonement whereas humans need not on the basis of the fact that God forgives as Judge, whereas humans (especially Christians) forgive as brethren. For God to forgive without atonement would abolish His governmental rule and contradict His holiness.

This atonement has been accomplished vicariously by Jesus Christ in behalf of the sinner. The Old Testament sacrifices pointed to this, and on the basis of it God was able to forgive prior to the cross. Actually, all forgiveness, both human and divine, is vicarious or substitutional. Whoever forgives *bears the debt himself*. On the human level a person bears the debt of an offense when he relinquishes his right to expect restitution of some sort from the person who has offended or injured him.

Now it is important to observe at this point that the guilt of an individual's sin against another cannot be transferred to someone else. Christ's ability to do this is no contradiction of the principle, for we must remember that He was not merely a third party but a member of the Godhead against whom man's offense rested. The fact remains that only the one offended can offer forgiveness. The implication of this in capital punishment will be seen shortly.

CHRIST AND FORGIVENESS

The gospels record numerous occasions on which Jesus forgave sin. For example, He forgave the man sick of palsy of his sins (Matt. 9:2, 5). The question arose among the Pharisees standing nearby as to Jesus' authority, and as Mark 2:7 records the same incident, they asked the legitimate question, "who can forgive sins but God alone?" To prove His authority and deity, Jesus healed the man. Now these "sins," let the reader note, were not crimes against the state, and Jesus was doing what only He as God had a right to do.

The classic example of Jesus' forgiving is found in John 8:1-11, a passage used frequently by abolitionists of the death penalty and alleged to be an example of Jesus' directly abolishing capital punishment. The story, of course, is of the woman arrested in the act of adultery, and under Mosaic law adultery was punishable by death (Lev. 20:10). Advocates of abolition claim that because Jesus did not invoke the death penalty, He was in effect abolishing capital punishment in principle. Since we have already considered this passage in detail, it is sufficient to point out that Jesus merely exercised His divine prerogative once again, refusing to fill the role of judge. John 8:1-11 is, then, an exposition of Jesus' willingness to forgive.

Jesus' *acts* of forgiving should be distinguished from His *teaching* on the subject. We cannot forgive as Jesus did, but we can follow His teaching, which is designed to set guidelines for us. In the so-called Lord's Prayer, Jesus taught His disciples to pray, "forgive us our debts, as we also have forgiven our debtors" (Matt. 6:12, KJV). Some commentators see a legalistic tone in this teaching and prefer to separate it from the Christian's ethic today. Most others prefer to harmonize it with later truth by seeing it in the attitude that must prevail on the part of Christians before they can rightly expect God's forgiveness, a forgiving attitude toward others. Whatever the case may be, the teaching involves forgiveness between individuals, not between the state and a convicted criminal.

Jesus' answer to Peter's question (Matt. 18:21) about how often he should forgive his brother is seen by some abolitionists as applicable to civil cases. Here again, it is a strange hermeneutic that applies an individual ethic to matters of civil government.

Matthew 5:38-39, in which Jesus sets aside the *lex talionis* and forbids retaliation, is used by some abolitionists in connection with their idea of the Christian's obligation to forgive, even though it does not teach anything about forgiveness directly. They believe that the Christian's refusal to resist evil involves his willingness to forgive. Logically, however, this would seem to lead consistently to refusing to punish *all* crime. Limiting the teaching to capital punishment only is purely arbitrary. It is more consistent to apply it as a personal—not civil— ethic.

THE CHRISTIAN'S OBLIGATION TO FORGIVE

The epistles of the New Testament, which are generally regarded as representing Christ's teachings applied to the church specifically, frequently enjoin believers to emulate the example of Christ. Romans 12:17-21 is an outstanding example of this. Paul's teaching here seems to echo that of the Sermon on the Mount. In this text forgiveness is not strictly the subject but rather a disposition to forgive. For a specific teaching on forgiveness one must resort to Ephesians 4:32: "And be kind to one another, tender-hearted, forgiving each other, just as God in Christ also has forgiven you." This implies that the Christian, who is asked to follow the example of Christ in many other ways, is, in the case of forgiveness, to take his own forgiveness by God as the basis for his action in this regard.

WHO CAN FORGIVE?

Based on the meaning of forgiveness, both in the human and divine realm, it is first of all clear that only the one who is offended or has suffered can bear the penalty of the offense. This is significant from at least two standpoints: (1) murder is uniquely an offense against God, therefore God must forgive it, and (2) murder, which violates the right to life of the one murdered, can be forgiven only by the one murdered, who, of course, is not available to do so.

In reference to the first assertion, the reader will recall that the original institution of capital punishment in Genesis 9:6 mentioned the offense to the image of God. Though this refers essentially to the value of human life, it also suggests the fact that God has been offended. David, who was directly responsible for the death of Uriah (2 Sam. 11:14-21), recognized this fact when he lamented, "Against Thee, Thee only, I have sinned" (Ps. 51:4). Though it might be argued that all sin is against God, it cannot be denied that murder is supremely so, because it violates not only God's law, but God's image. No man, much less society, can therefore "forgive" such an offense.

In reference to the second assertion, Christ teaches us that we can forgive only those who have wronged us personally. In the case of murder, the victim, who only has the right to forgive, is dead. It is true that men offer forgiveness to men when the gospel is preached, and perhaps this is where those who would forgive the murderer confuse the issue. They seem to fail to realize that preachers of reconciliation are, first of all, responding to a specific mandate that involves the right to offer God's forgiveness to the sinner for all his sins upon his repentance (2 Cor. 5:20-21). Second, they seem to confuse the kind of forgiveness that is offered in a spiritual sense with the kind of forgiveness that individuals can offer one another on earth. The former kind settles the issue with God; the latter may settle the issue with men. Though the issue may be settled with God so that condemnation is removed and eternal life is received by the repentant sinner, the temporal consequences of his sins may continue on, as it was in the case of David's sin with Bathsheba. Few among the abolitionists who argue on the basis of this principle of forgiveness are willing to apply it so consistently that the murderer is allowed to go free without any punishment at all. It appears that what they really want to offer is a kind of *leniency.* Let them, therefore, rest their appeal on some other basis than biblical forgiveness.

15
The Relation of Capital Punishment to Expiation

Referring to Genesis 9:6, one writer has claimed that the death of the murderer is expiatory.[1] This argument also involves the question of the progress of revelation as it relates to the meaning of the death of Christ. In the Old Testament, the Levitical sacrifices were clearly expiatory; that is, they were sacrifices that atoned for sin. These sacrifices are generally recognized by evangelical scholars as being typical of the death of Christ and thus pointing to the conclusion that the death of Christ was expiatory also.

Now it is necessary, in order to connect capital punishment in some way with the idea of expiation, to interpret Genesis 9:6 as involving some kind of expiation. Since the expiatory sacrifices were done away by the death of Christ, we are to infer that capital punishment, also an expiatory sacrifice, was thus done away by the death of Christ.

1. See A. B. Rhodes et. al., "The Bible and Capital Punishment," *Eternity* 12 (June 1961): 17-18; John Howard Yoder, "Capital Punishment and the Bible," *Christianity Today* 4 (1 February 1969): 5.

Frequently, such other Old Testament passages involving capital punishment as Numbers 35:33 are cited: "So you shall not pollute the land in which you are; for blood pollutes the land and no expiation can be made for the land for the blood that is shed on it, except by the blood of him who shed it."

The Meaning of Expiation

The Hebrew word *kaphar* probably means to cover or to wash away. The Greek equivalent, *hilasmos,* translated "expiation" or "propitiation," is basically the same in meaning as the Hebrew, "the setting aside of sin as guilt against God."[2]

Either God or man can be involved in expiation. For example, in the Old Testament, men offered sacrifices of various sorts to expiate for their sins. These sacrifices were required by God and were typical of the sacrifice of Jesus Christ yet to come. On the other hand, God Himself expiates for the sin of man in a final sense by offering up Christ on the cross (1 John 2:2).

The Irrelevance of the Issue

Those who say that capital punishment is expiatory—and therefore fulfilled and done away by the expiation of Christ just like the other expiatory sacrifices of the Old Testament—err in at least two ways. First of all, though expiation is not explicit in Genesis 9:1-6, it might be admitted from other later passages such as Numbers 35:31-33 that there was a kind of expiation involved in capital punishment, at least at that point. However, there are other facets of Genesis 9:6, and to ignore such things

2. See William F. Arndt and F. Wilbur Gingrich, *A Greek-English Lexicon of the New Testament* (Chicago: U. of Chicago, 1957), p. 376; *Theological Dictionary of the New Testament,* s.v. ἱλασμός [hilasmos].

as deterrence and justice is either dishonest or faulty exegesis. Capital punishment might have been done away with if it served only the purpose of expiation in this sense.

Second, those who allege that capital punishment was expiatory fail to recognize that there is a difference between expiatory sacrifice and expiatory punishment. Punishment is necessarily connected with wrongdoing and guilt. It can only be justified as the expiation or satisfaction for guilt. In other words, when a crime is committed under civil law, an expiation to the law or society is necessarily made in the form of a prescribed punishment. The law is "satisfied" when the offender suffers his punishment (expiates for his crime).

However, when an expiatory sacrifice was made in the Old Testament, the victim was not "punished" in any way for sins it had committed; rather, the victim took the punishment due the one offering it. This is substitutionary and therefore is typical of Christ's sacrifice. Capital punishment was in no way typical of the sacrifice of Christ, even though Christ suffered His death under a law demanding capital punishment, for it involved the punishment of one who was guilty of His crime. Christ assumed as a substitute the guilt of the human race, but He could do this only because He was sinless or guiltless. For capital punishment to have been fulfilled in the sacrifice of Christ, therefore, it would have to have been typical.

In order to be consistent, those who hold to the expiatory sacrifice fulfilled by the death of Christ would have to hold that all forms of punishment under civil law were abolished. Certainly none of them can be accused of this. In the Mosaic legislation, both expiatory sacrifices and civil ordinances appear. Each had its function, one in the spiritual realm and the other in the civil realm. The death penalty has its proper place in the civil realm under civil legislation, whereas the typical sacrifices, given to provide a way for dealing with the sin question and maintaining Israel's relationship with God and at the same time pointing to Christ, had their place in the ceremonial ordinances. This distinction must be maintained or the result is the kind of confusion involved in the expiatory view of capital punishment.

Conclusion:
The Unpleasant Necessity

The revulsion which the punishment of death creates in the mind and feelings of every human being is natural. But, ultimately, many unpleasant facts of life are to be traced to the Fall of man and are, because of the effects of that fall upon man's nature and environment, necessary evils. Capital punishment, by its very nature, is awful, but so is judgment of any kind. Yet judgment must be meted out, not only in God's divine administration but also in man's civil administration, which is really an extension of the divine rule. Life and death and judgment that involves life and death are indeed the prerogatives of God, but such a prerogative has clearly been delegated to man in order that he might have a basis on which to maintain law and order. In theology, this delegation of power is part of common grace. Fallen man is restrained by certain gracious provisions of God so that his sinful nature might not carry him into utter chaos and anarchy. Civil government is one of these gracious provisions, and capital punishment is vital to civil government, especially when extended to insurrection.

Among most opponents to the death penalty, the principal point of departure from traditional concepts of justice has been lack of regard for Scripture. Most modern theology has tended to seek other norms and standards for authority than the Bible, and these standards have usually been centered in man's feelings and reason. For evangelical Christians, however, the Scriptures continue to be the source book of theology and the absolute standard by which everything else is to be judged. It is to this minority that such a book as this will have an appeal. To them, the issue of capital punishment will be resolved by what the Bible teaches.

But the problem has been, what does the Bible teach? Everyone recognizes a change in God's dealings with man over the period of redemptive history. We have attempted to deal with this problem in regard to capital punishment and have concluded that progressive revelation has not altered the original mandate of Genesis 9:6. This feature of that original arrangement of affairs has been reincorporated into the economy in which we live today by virture of certain unchanging features such as the sinful nature of man, which originally gave rise to it. The apparent conflict of the teachings of Christ on love and forgiveness and His death, which abolished the law system, do not have any effect on the institution of human government of which capital punishment is a part.

Now the very problem of human sin, which creates the need for capital punishment, implies the purpose of capital punishment, the establishing of the principle of retributive justice, the maintenance of the sanctity of life, and the deterrence of further crime. Redemption itself is based upon the satisfaction of justice in retribution, and the death penalty is essentially an expression of retribution on the human plane. The rejection of retribution as a valid and necessary principle in justice touches upon the very need for Christ's death on the cross. It is at this point, especially, that a man's view of capital punishment, reflects his concept of the death of Christ consistently carried out in its implications.

The present state of affairs in which lawlessness has reached a historical peak is merely the result of men's failure to respect the biblical teachings on justice. The question of capital punishment may seem to be relatively insignificant before the awesome problems of our twentieth-century civilization, but it is closely involved with the weaknesses in modern man's thinking. Today men seem to find it increasingly difficult to make hard decisions, as though the moral thrust of a given situation is not clear to them. It is hoped that this book may make a contribution toward setting forth the moral significance of the issue of capital punishment by exposure to the biblical revelation.

Index of Subjects

Index of Persons

Index of Scripture